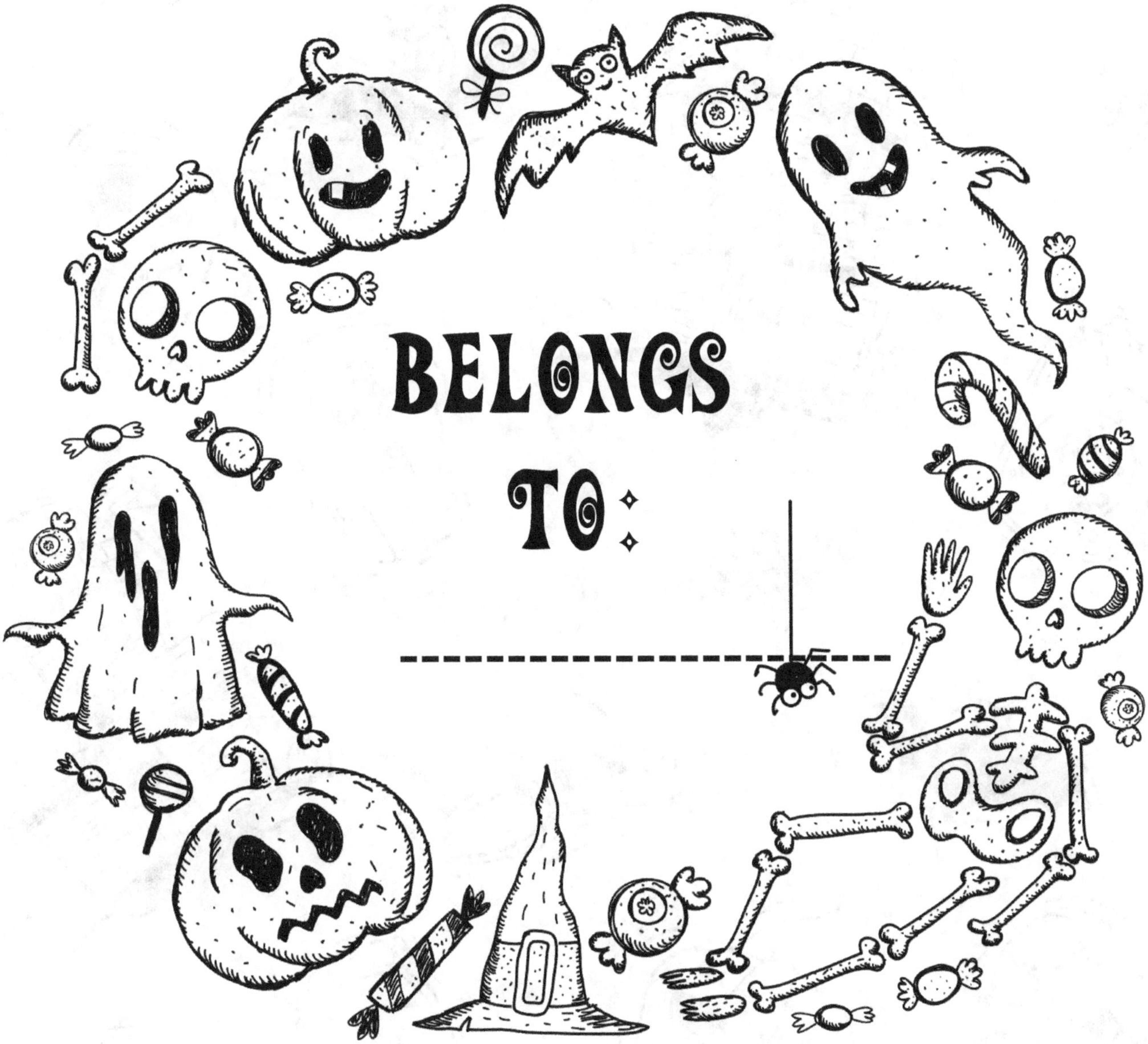

BELONGS TO:

_____

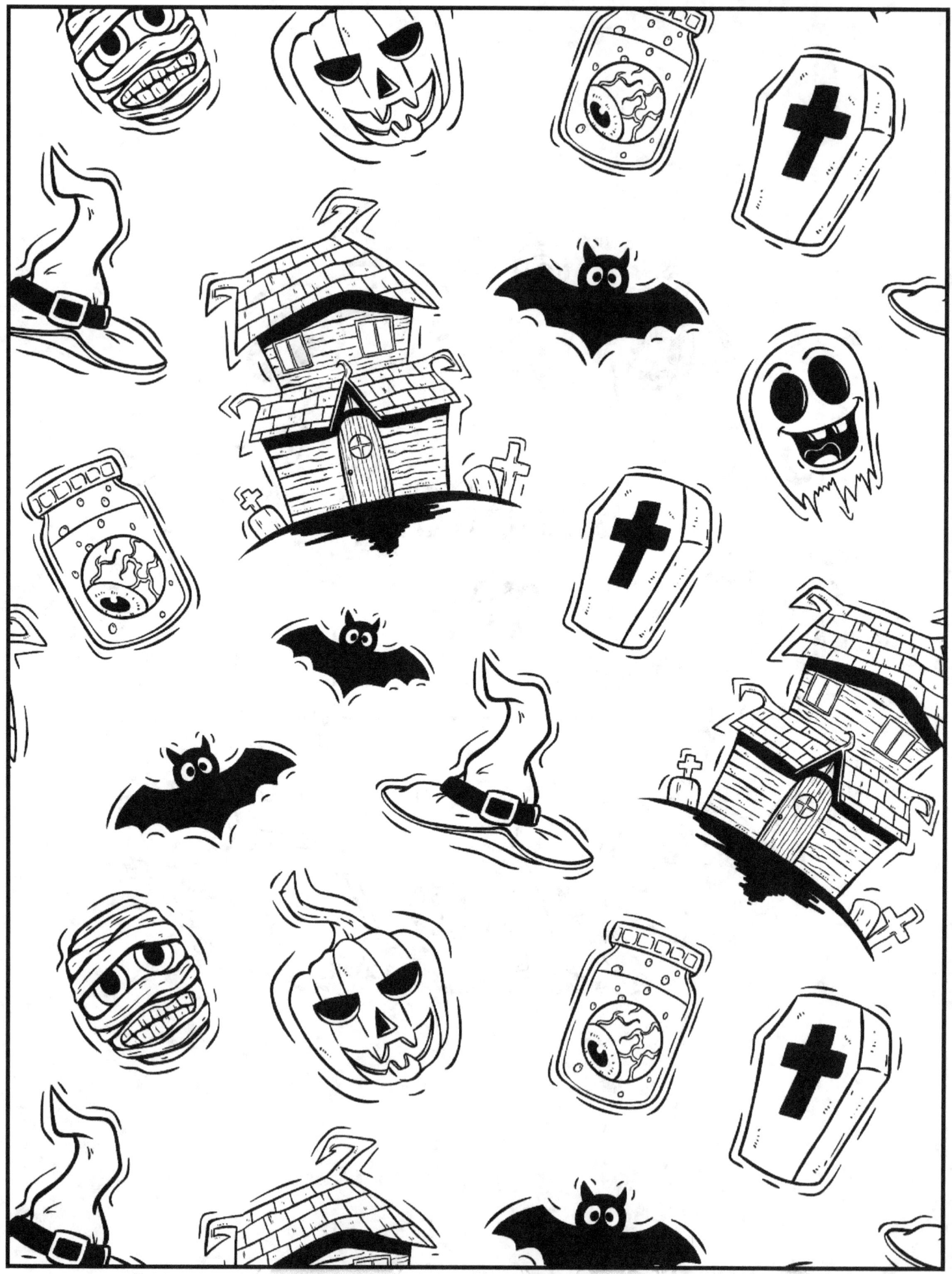

Dedication

This book is for you, dear Colorist.

"May your time spent coloring these pages bring you joy, plus lots of fun mixed in with plenty of relaxation.."

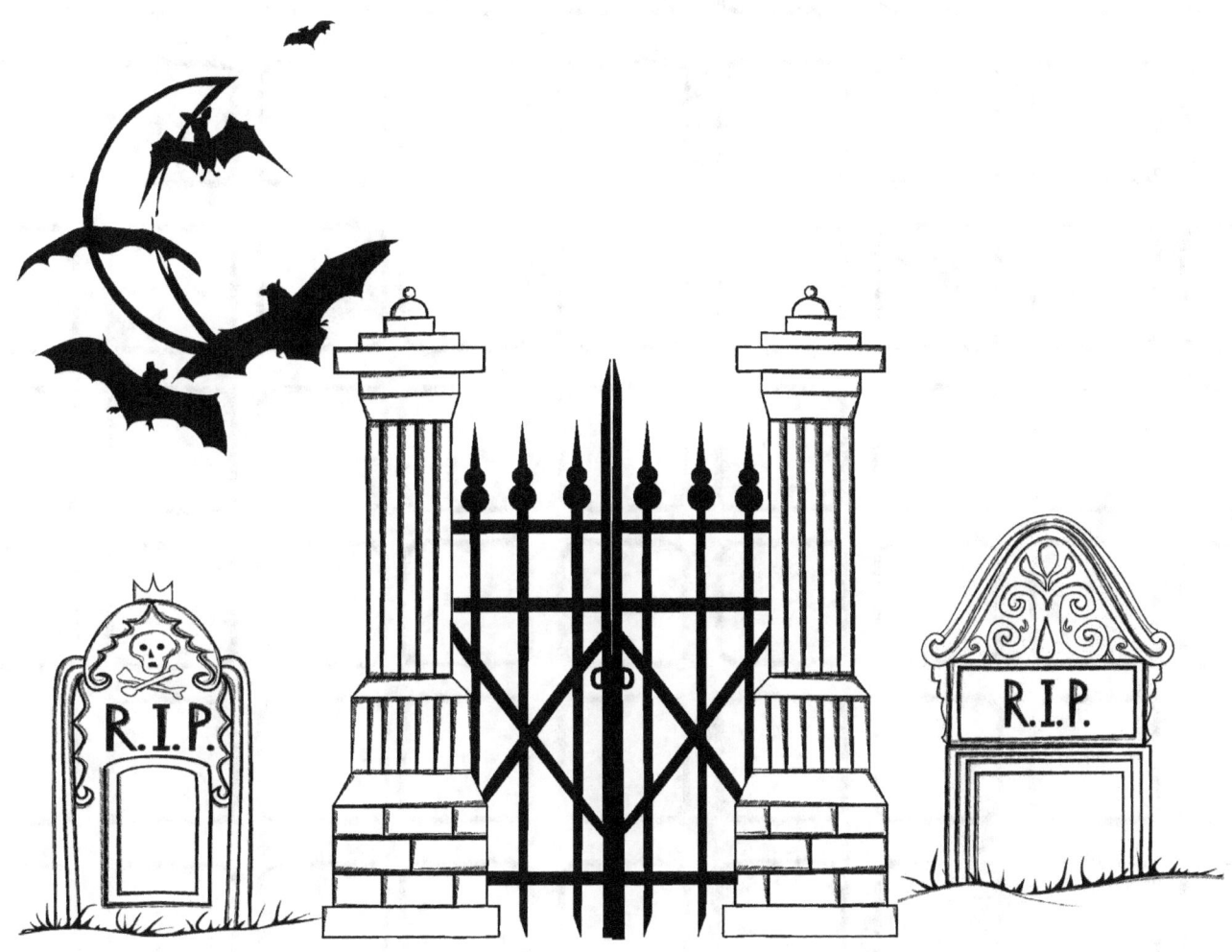

Copyright © 2020 Kreative Kolor - All Rights Reserved

No part of this publication may be reproduced, stored in a retrieval system, or transmitted in any form or by any means, electronic, mechanical, photocopying, recording or otherwise, without the prior written permission of the publisher.

COLOR TESTER

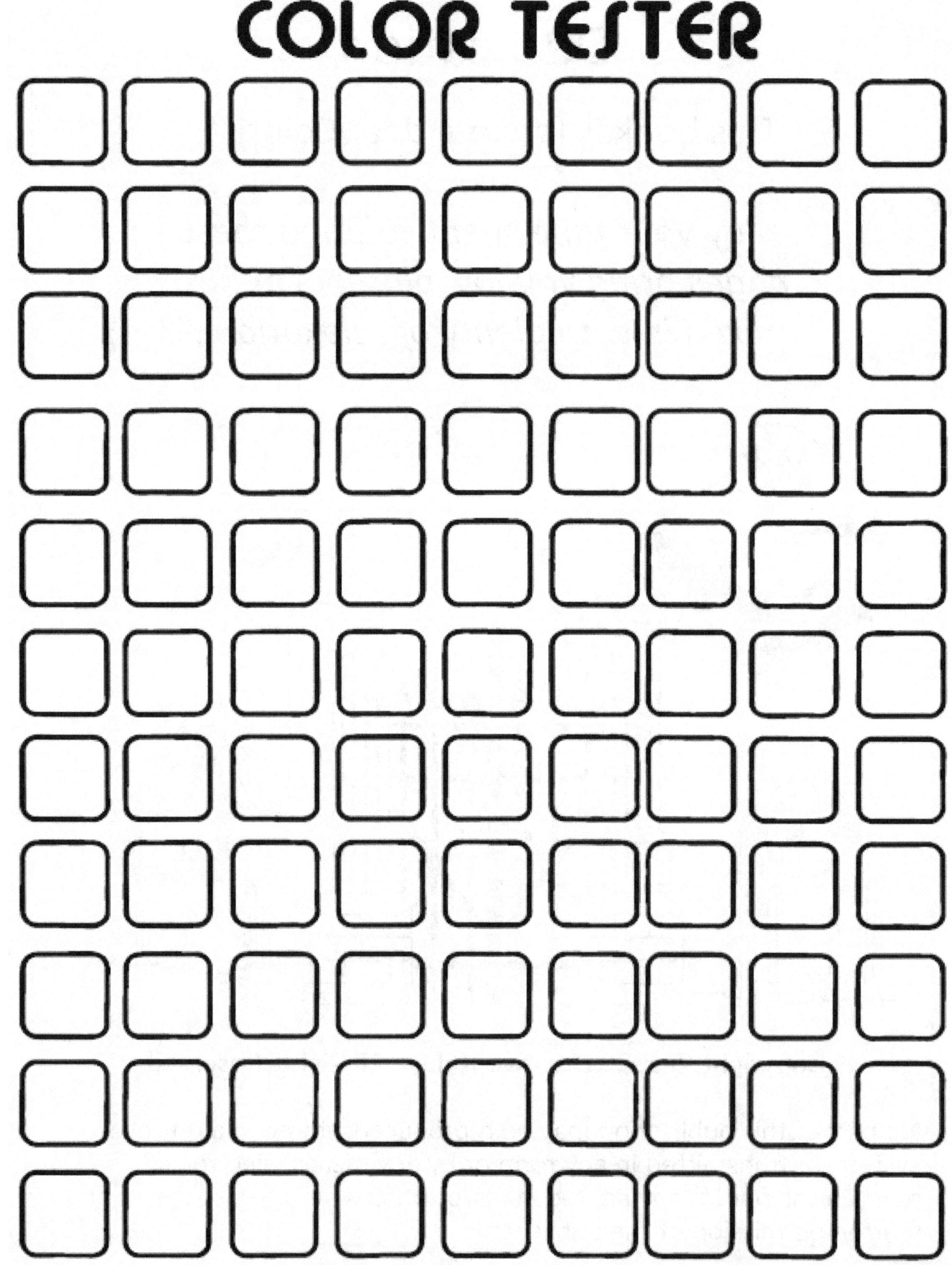

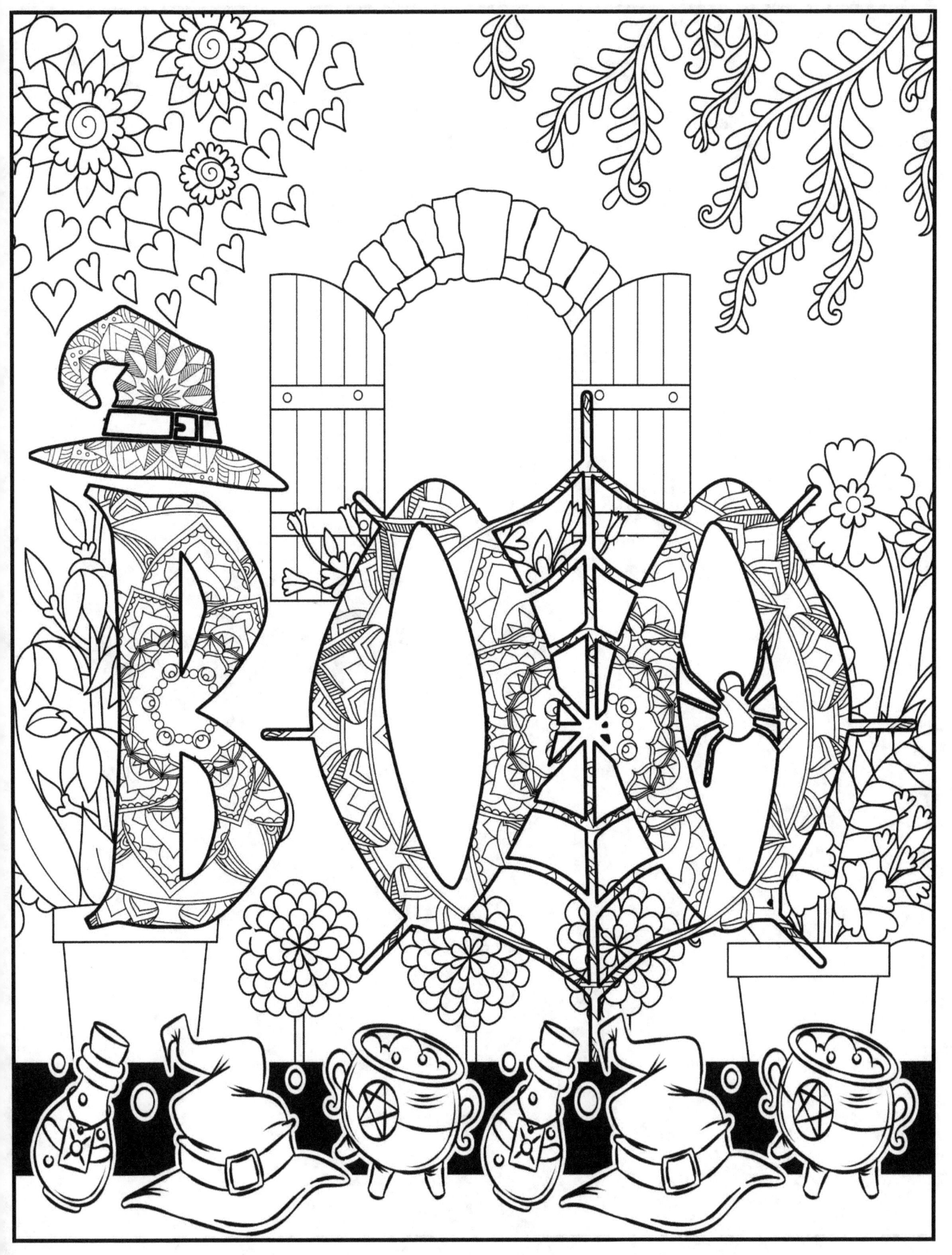

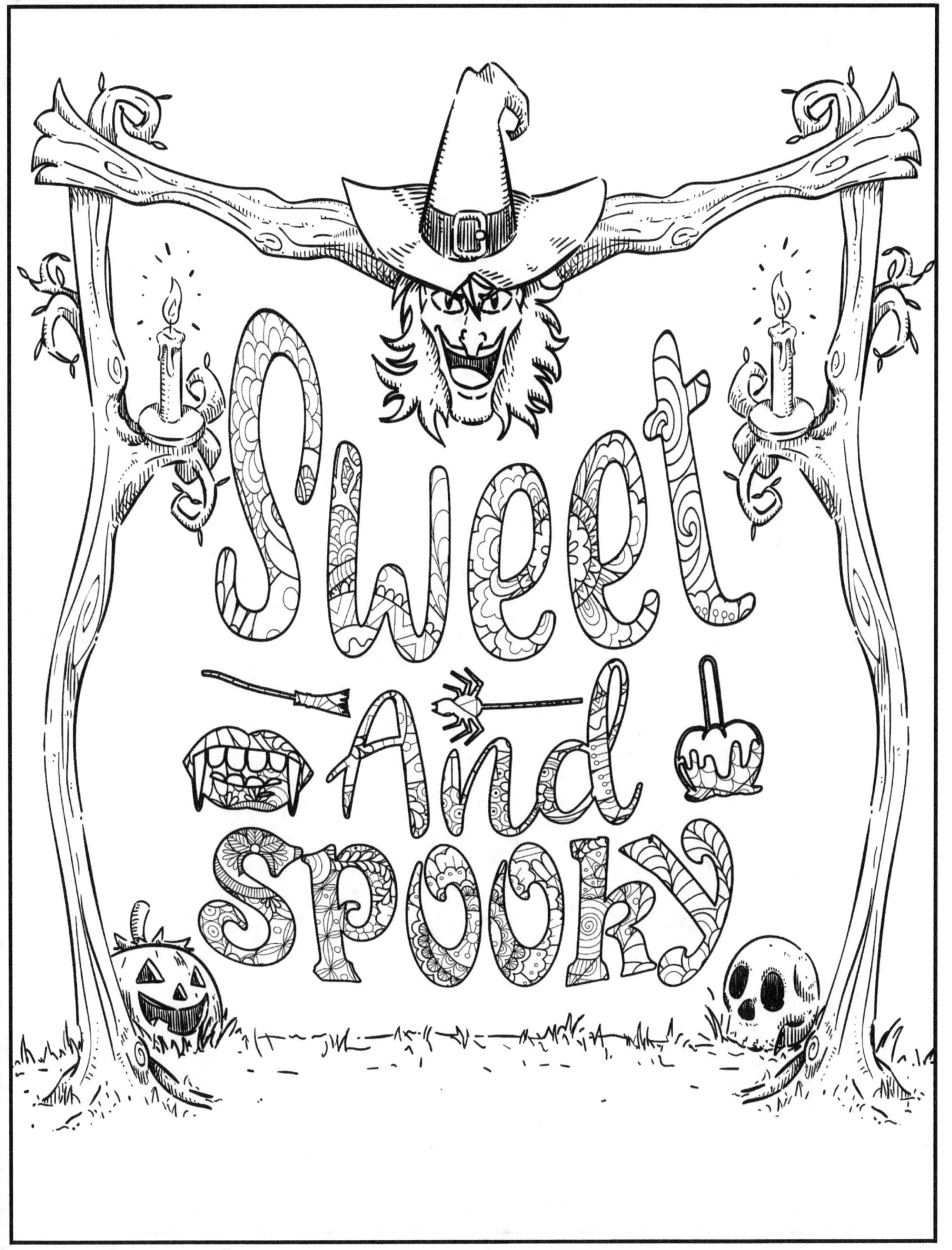

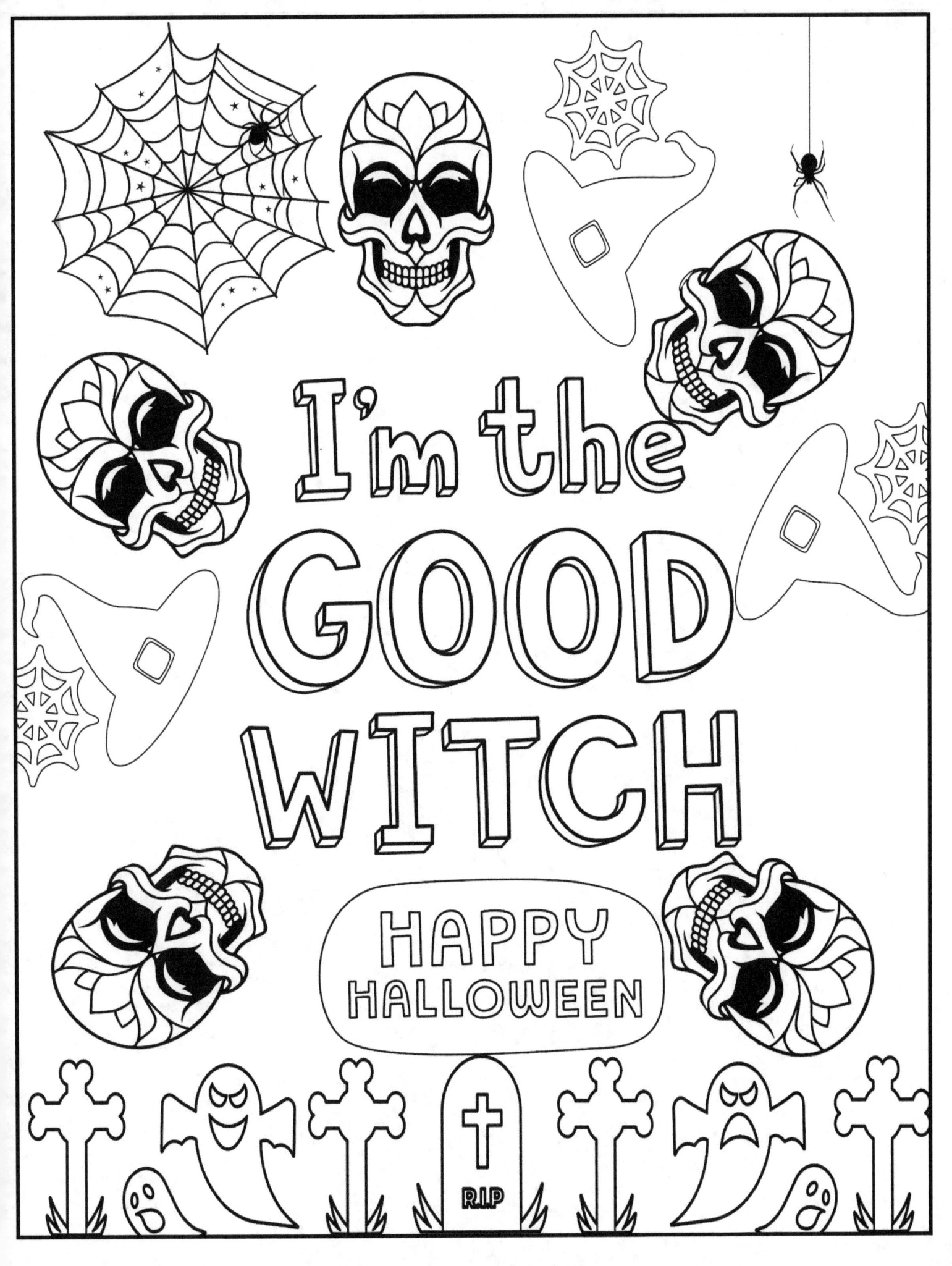

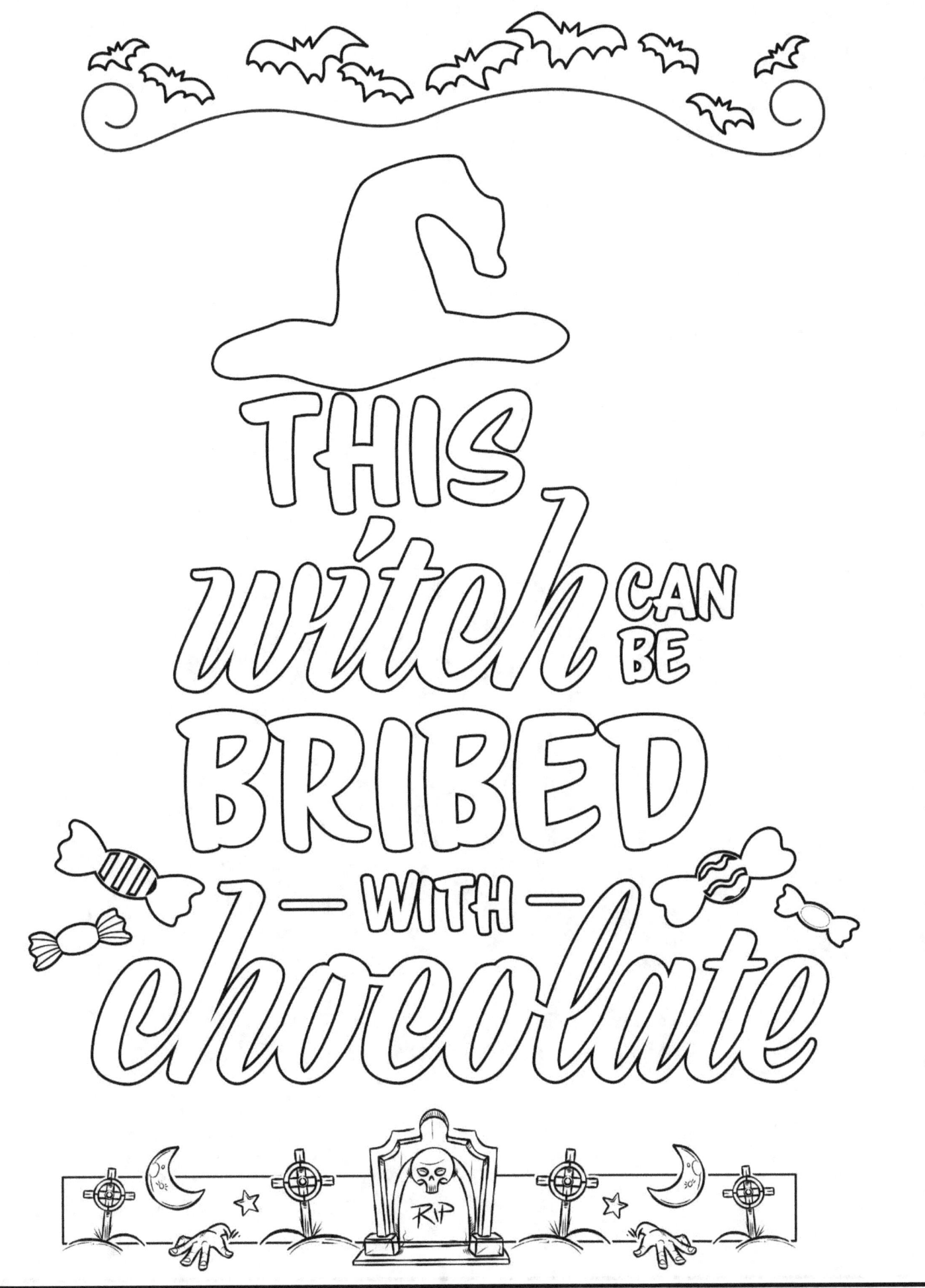

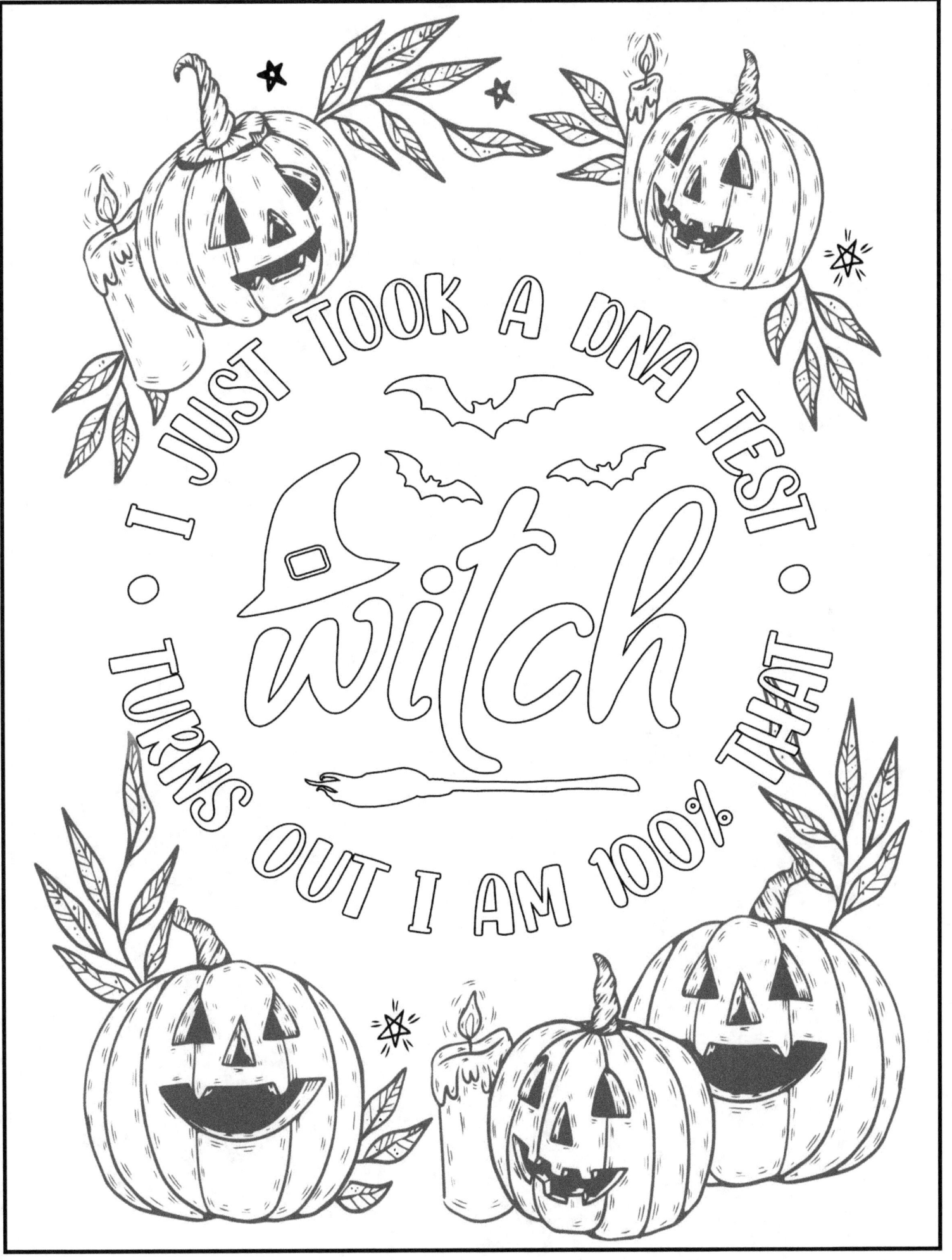

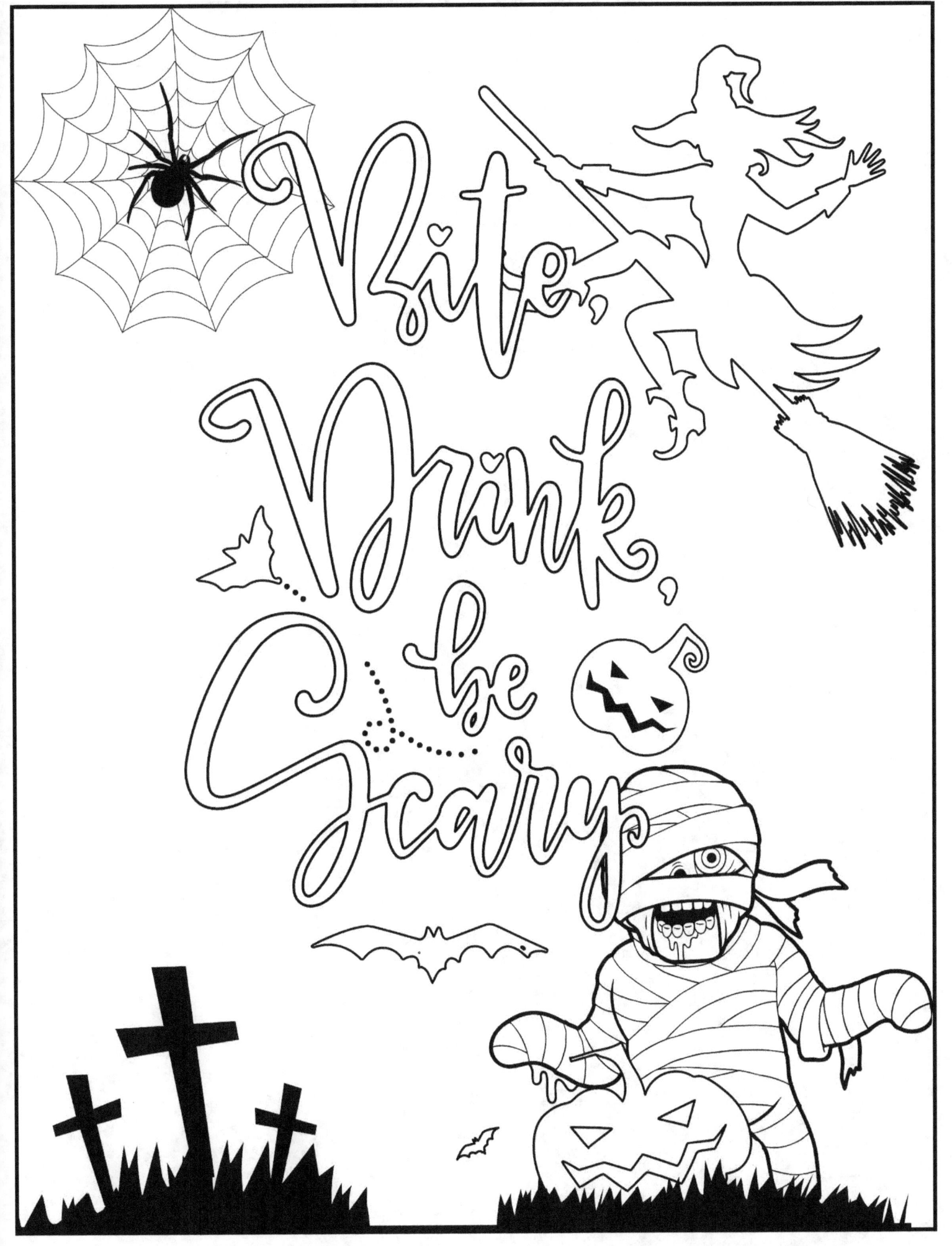

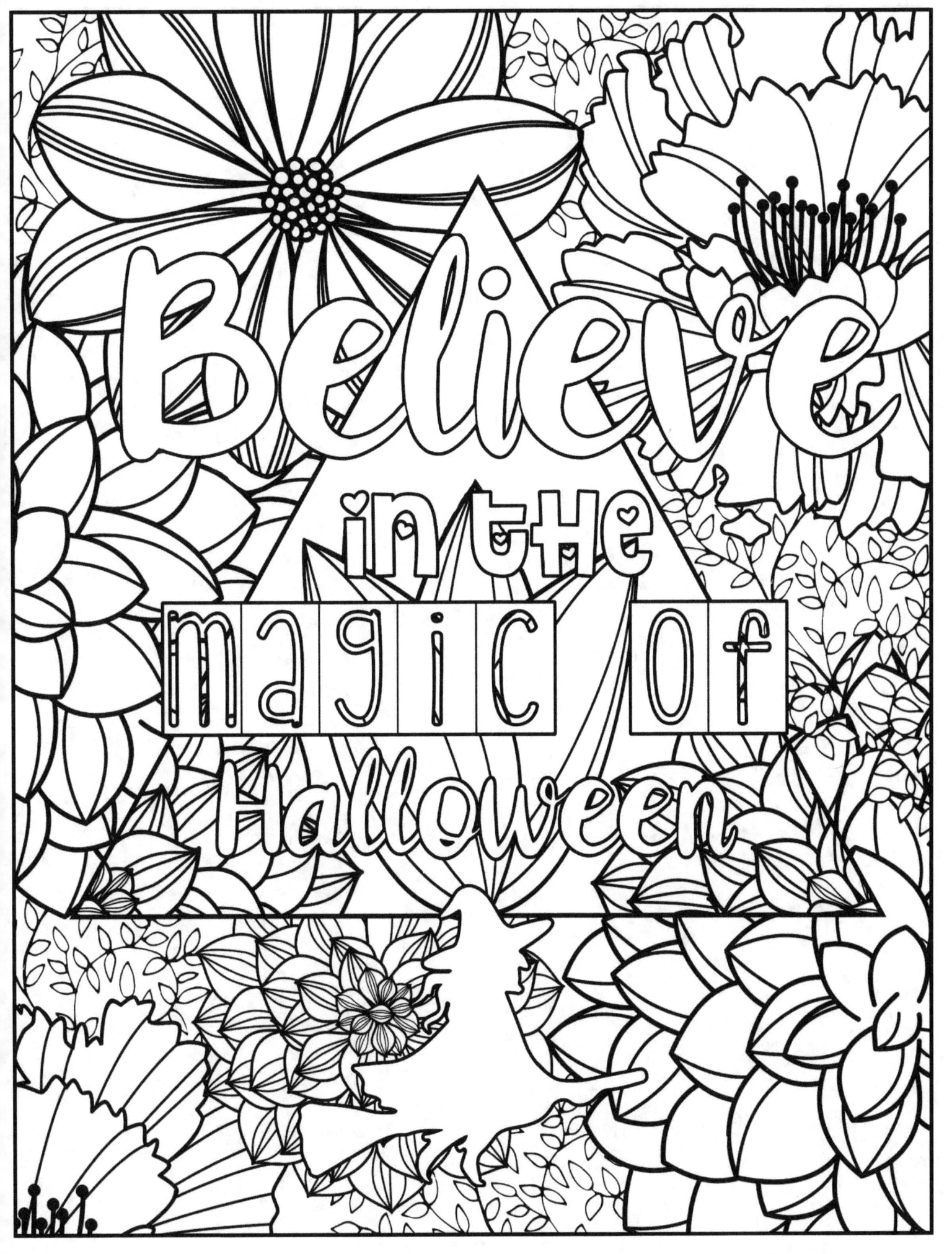

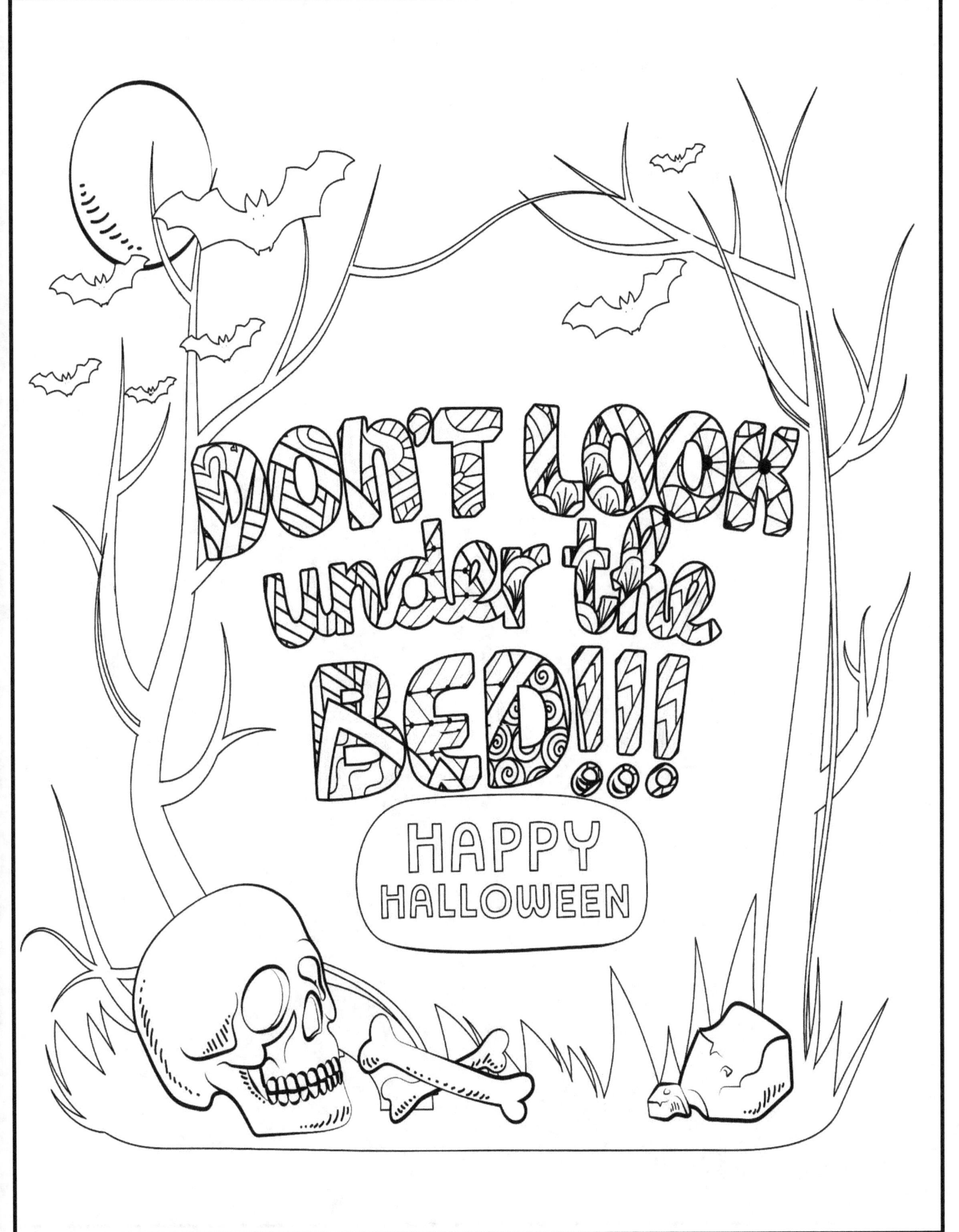

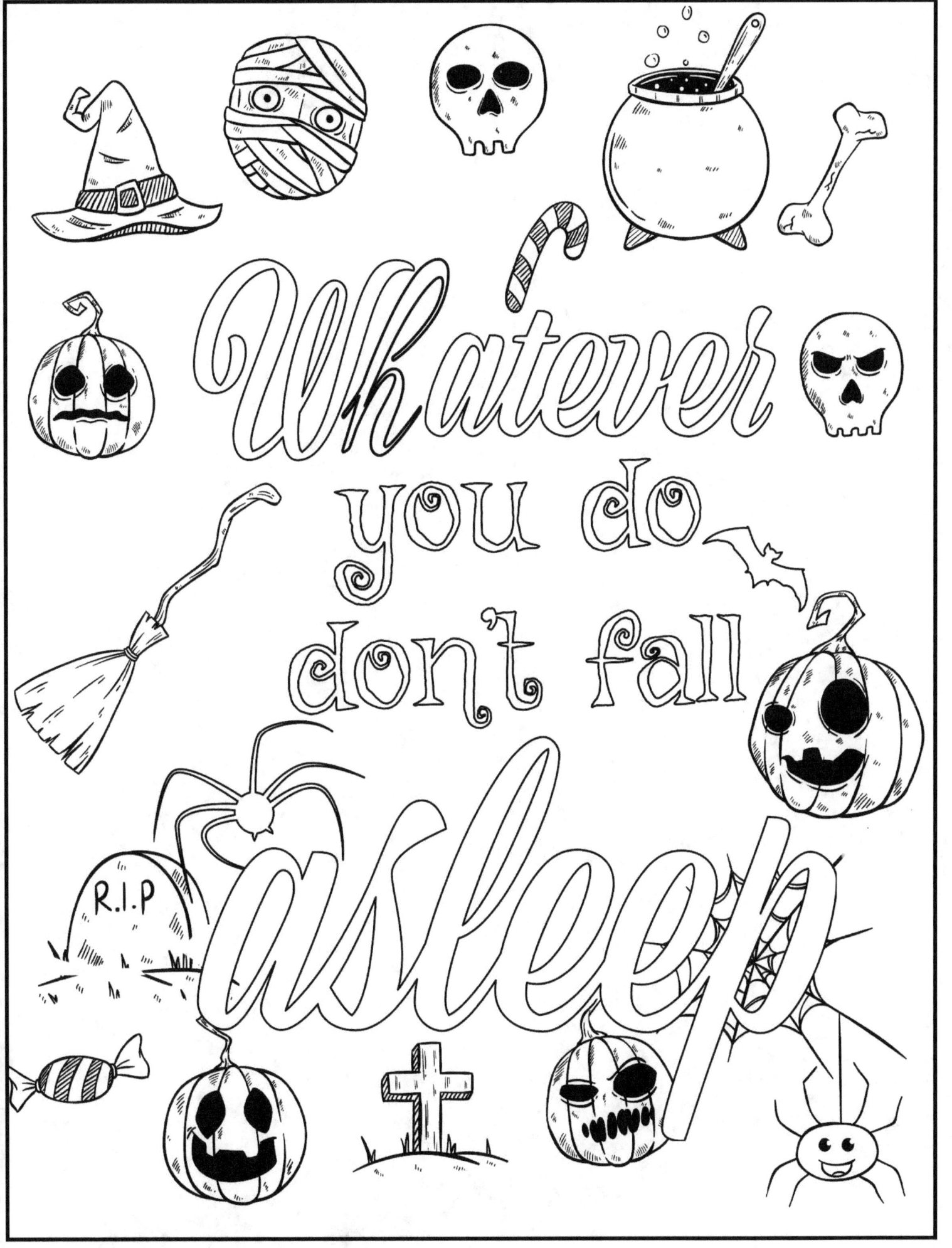

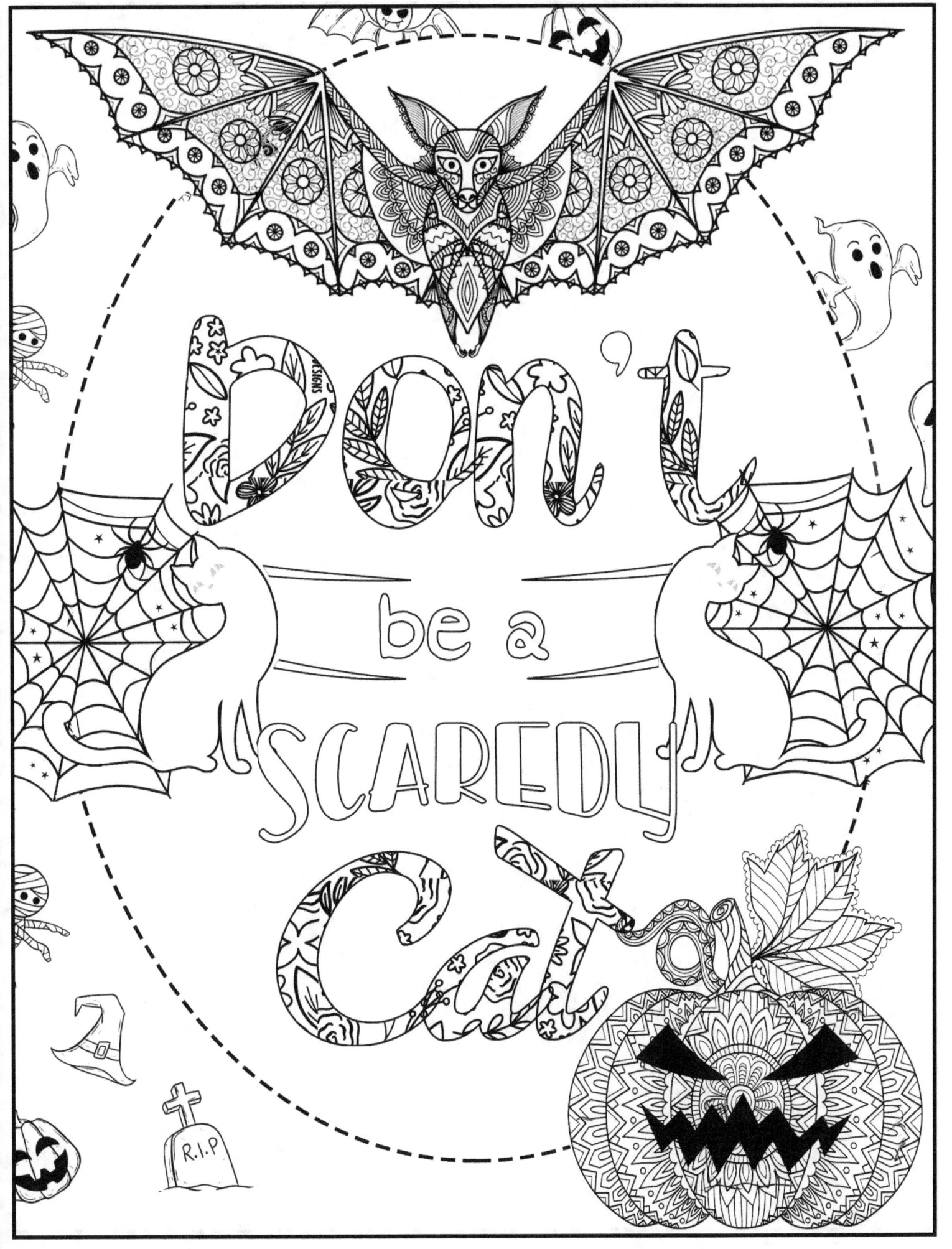

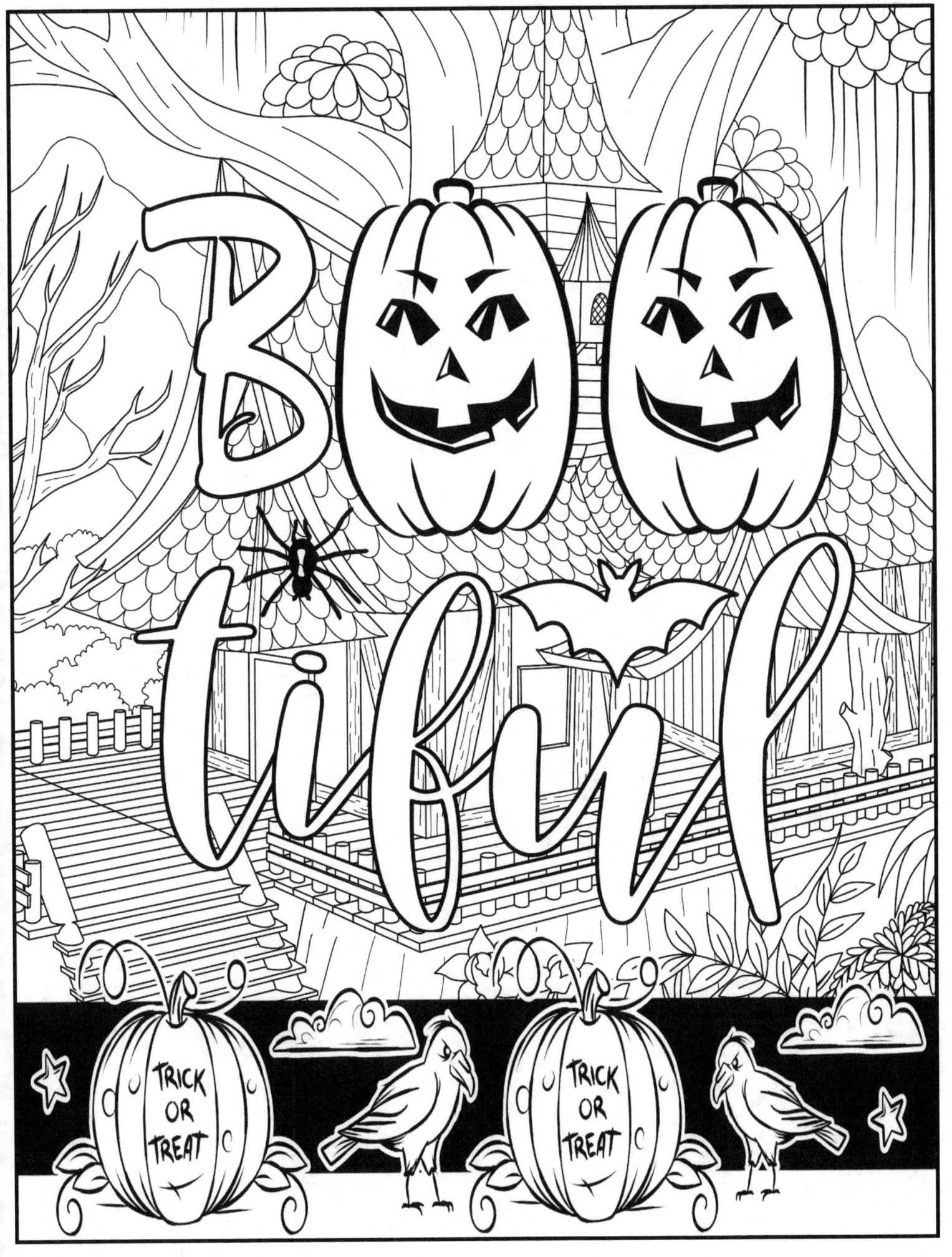

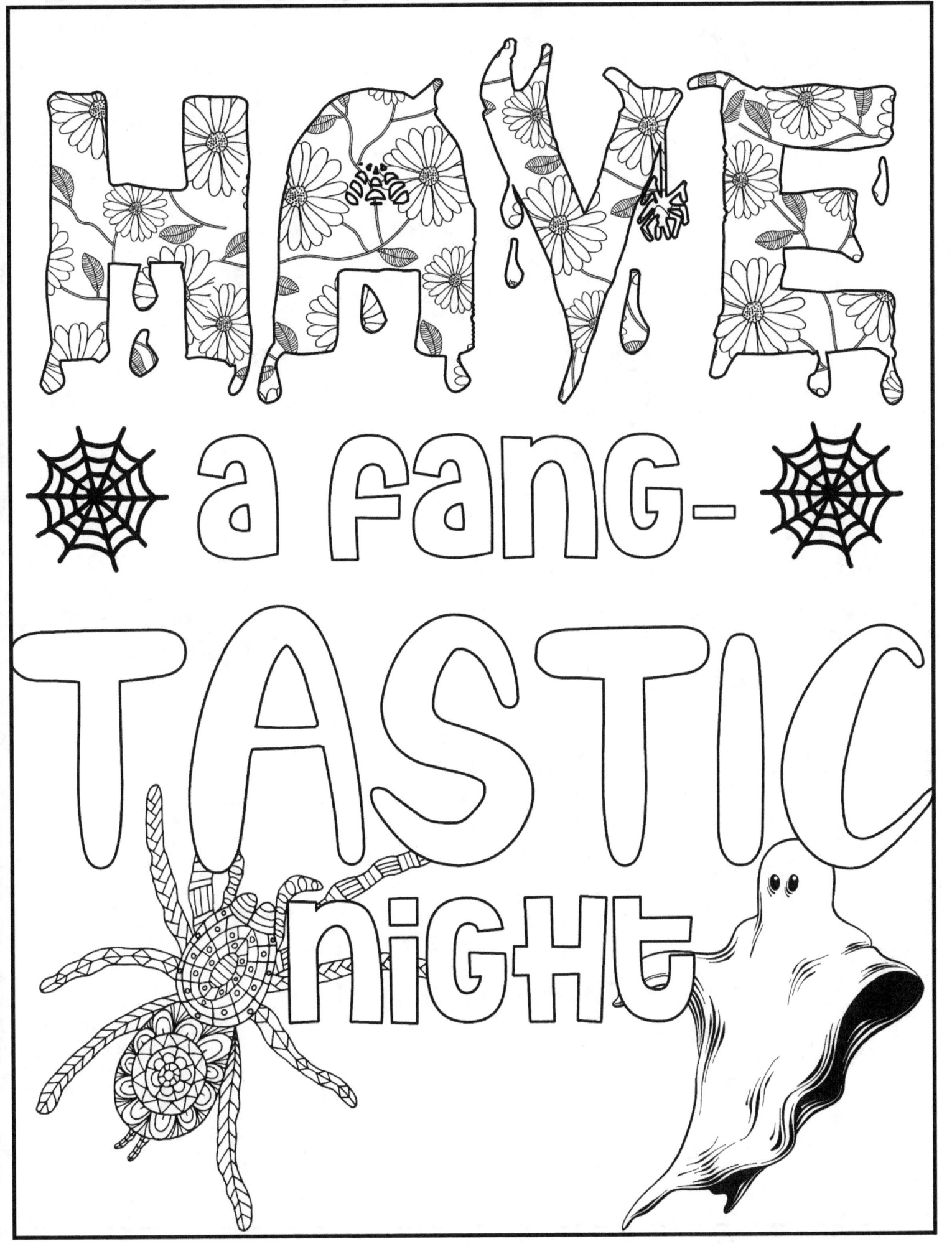

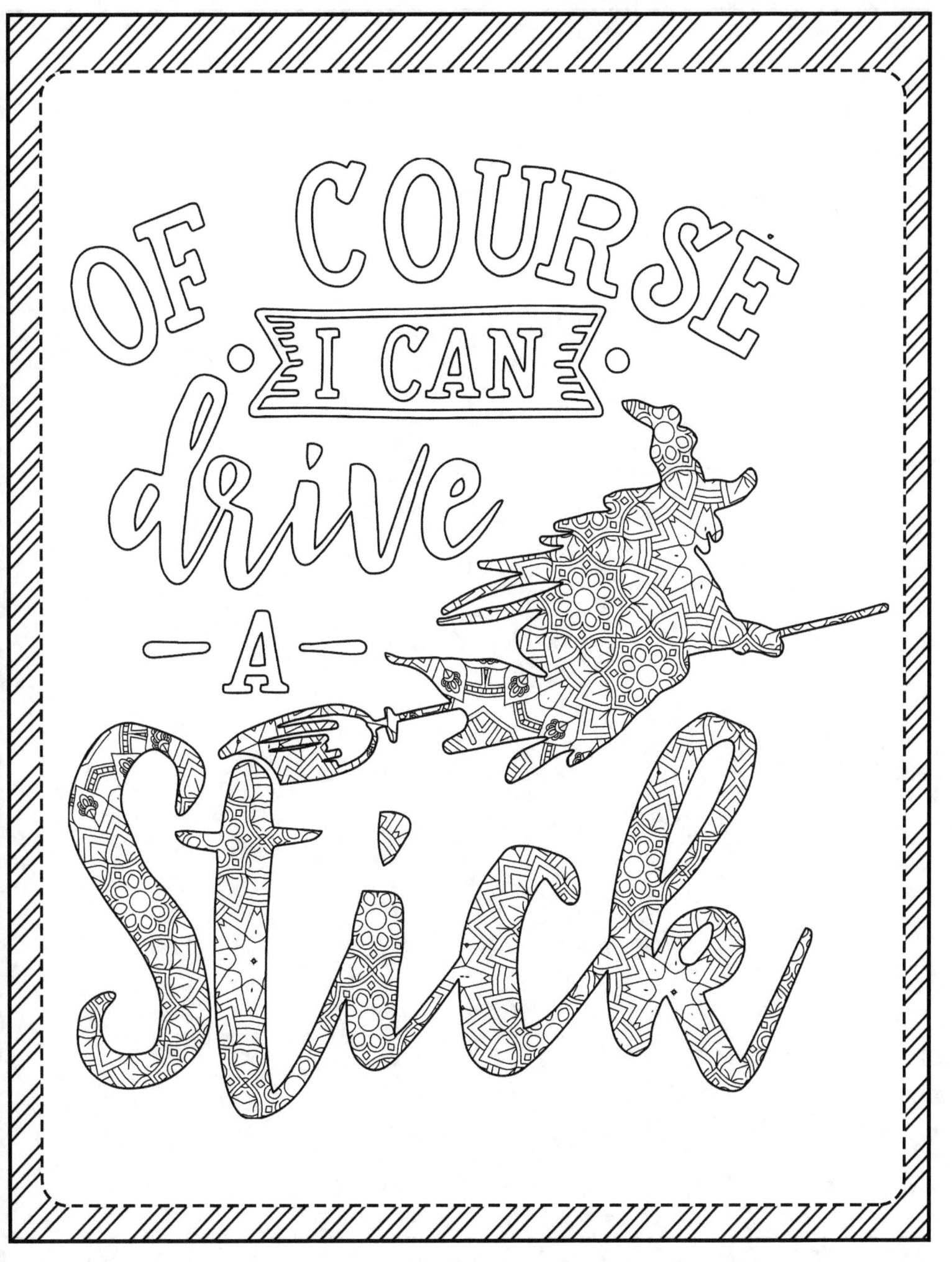

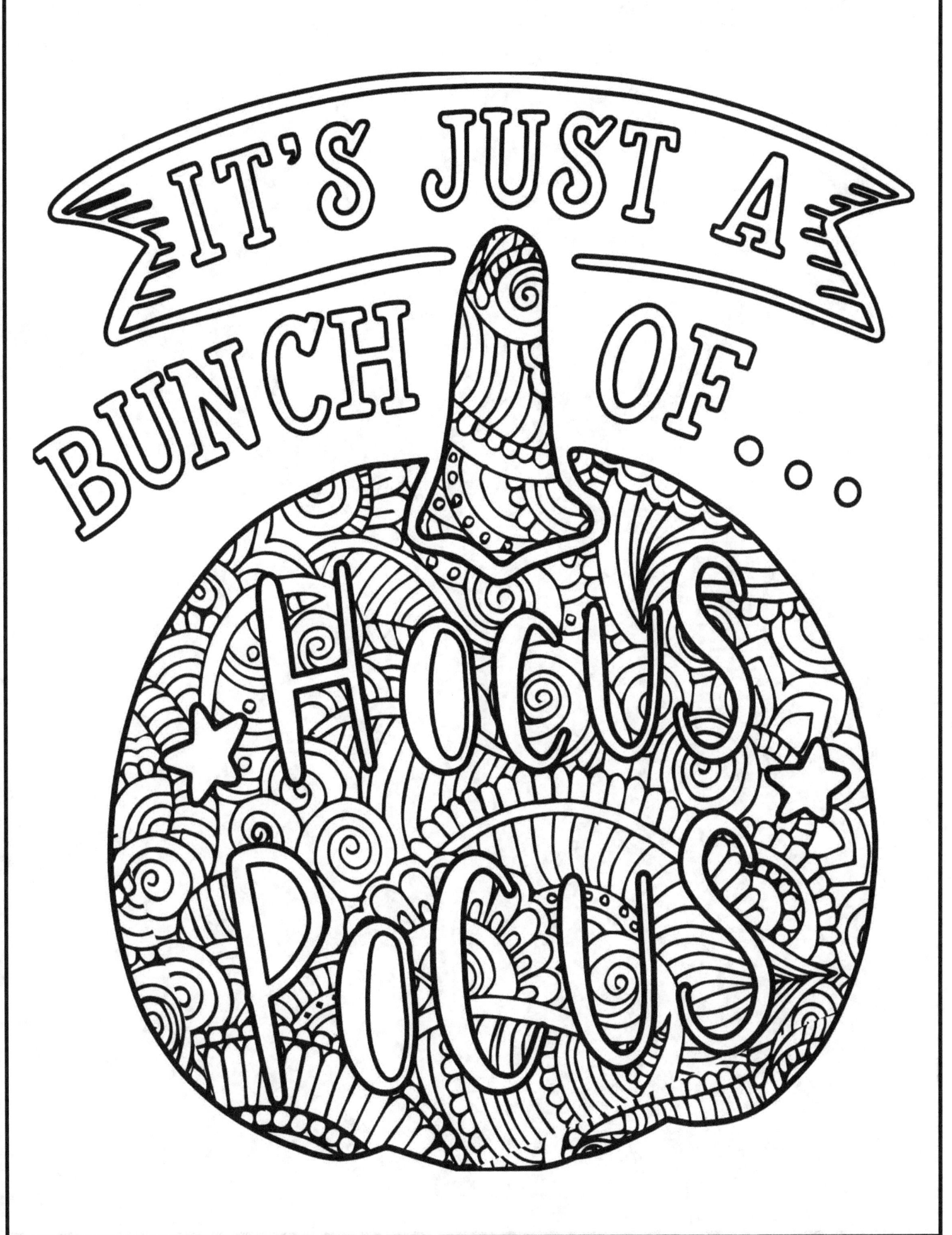

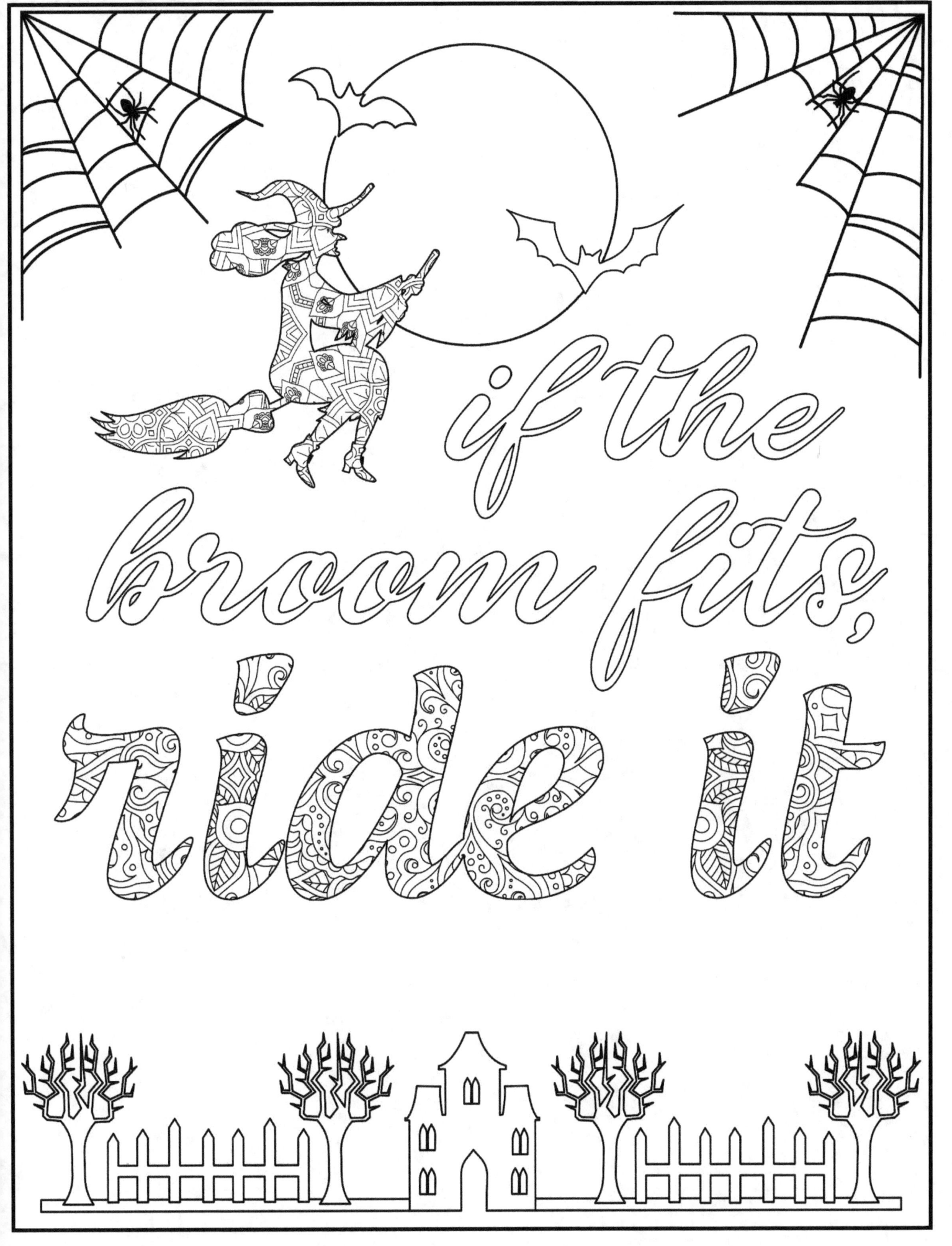

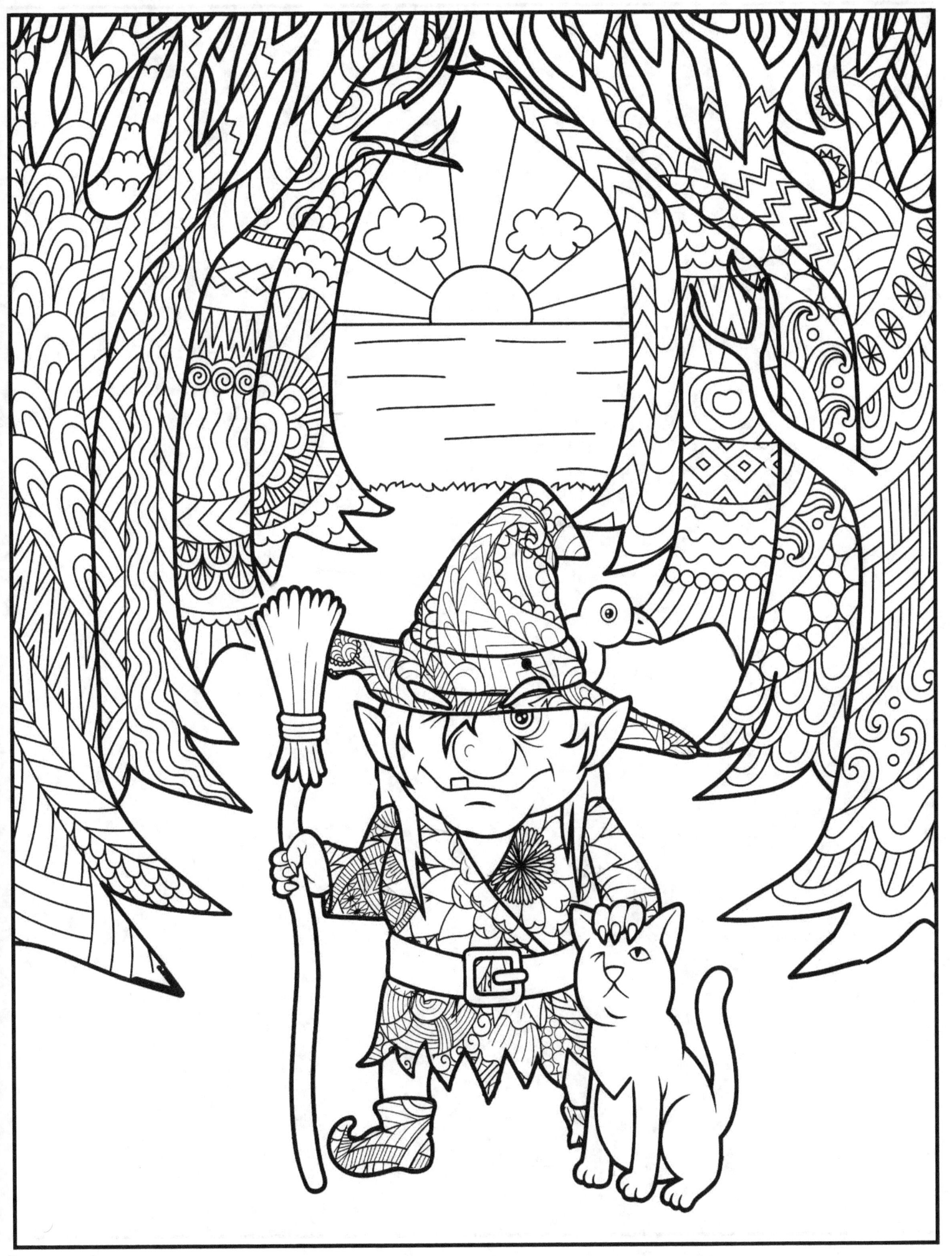

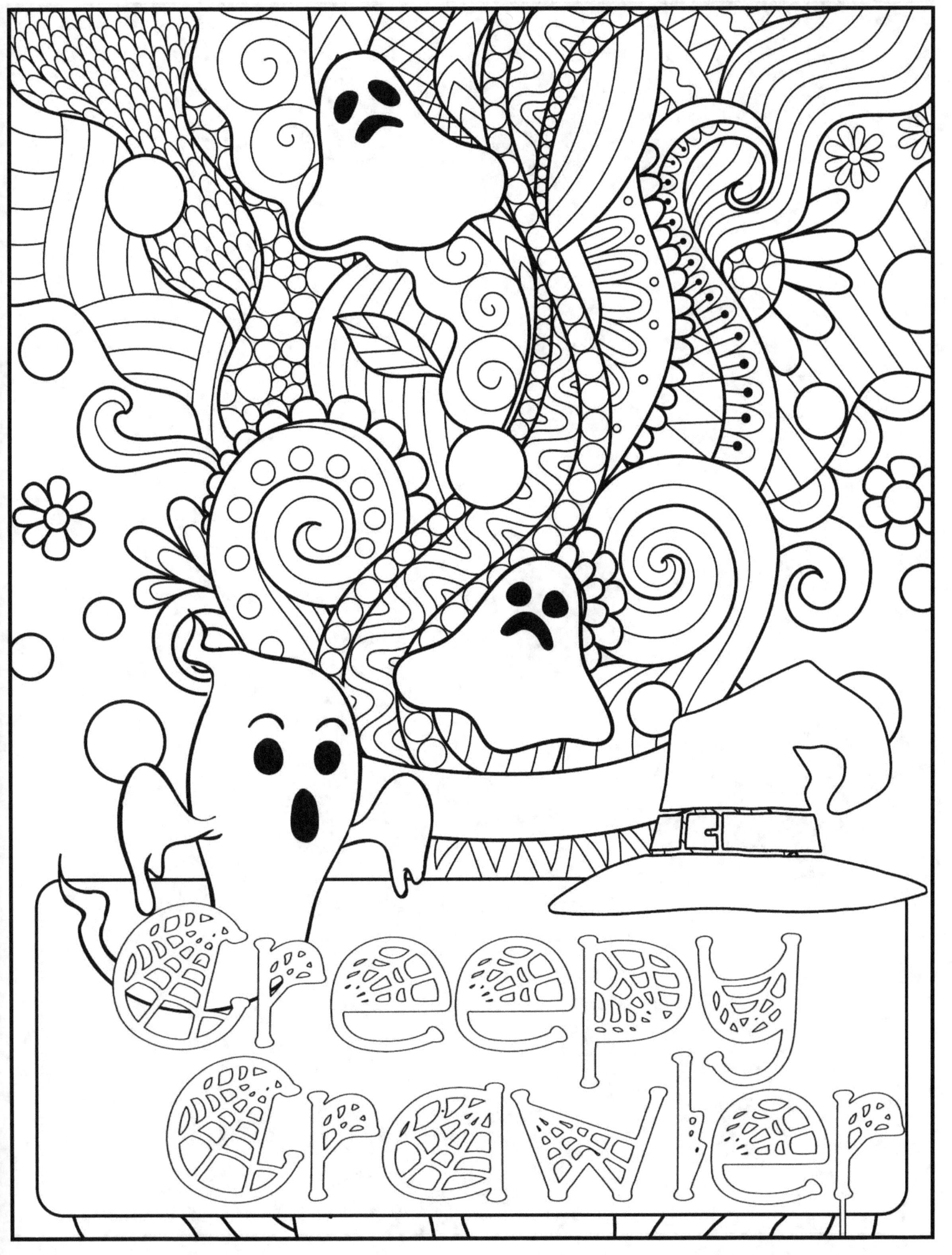

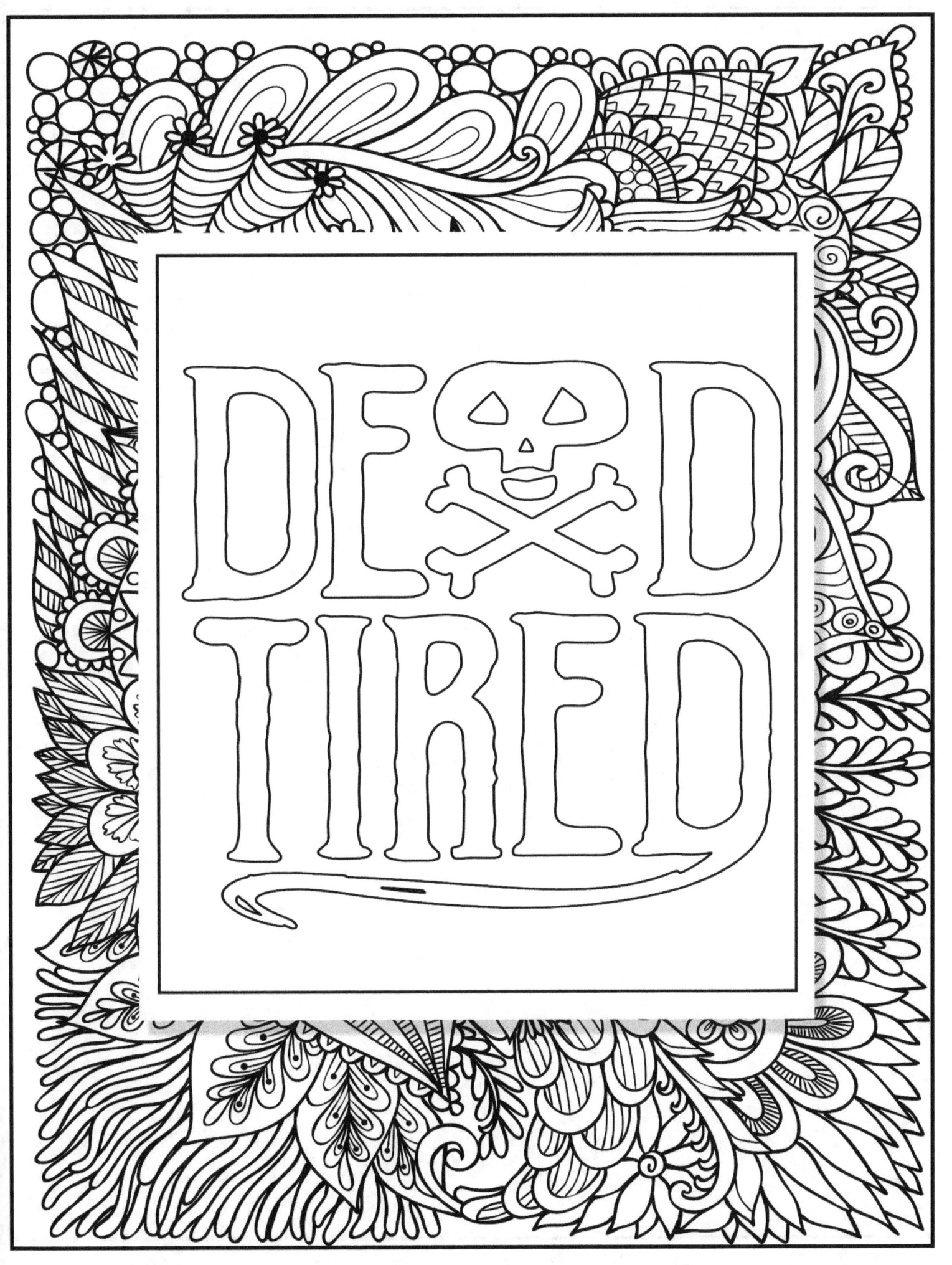

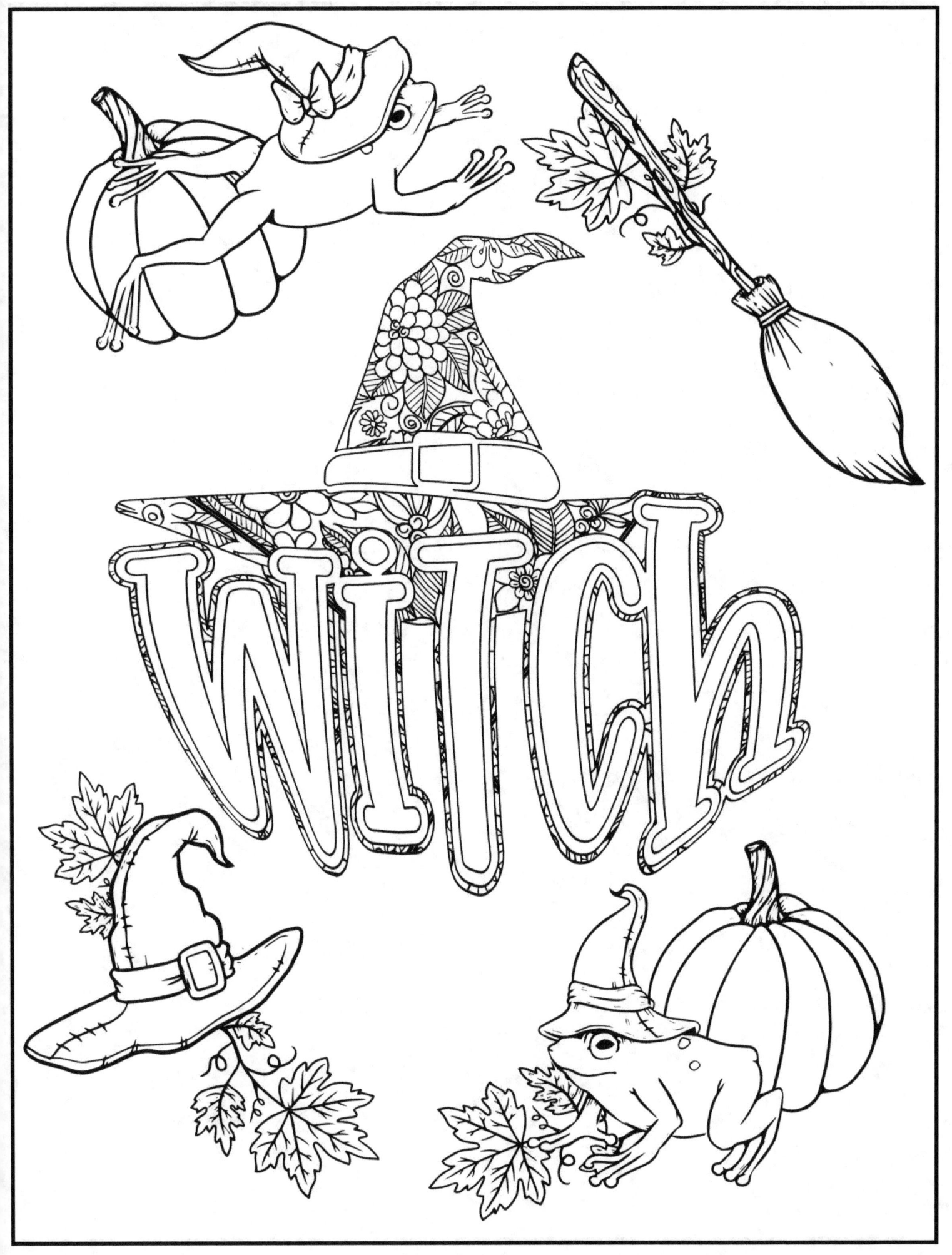

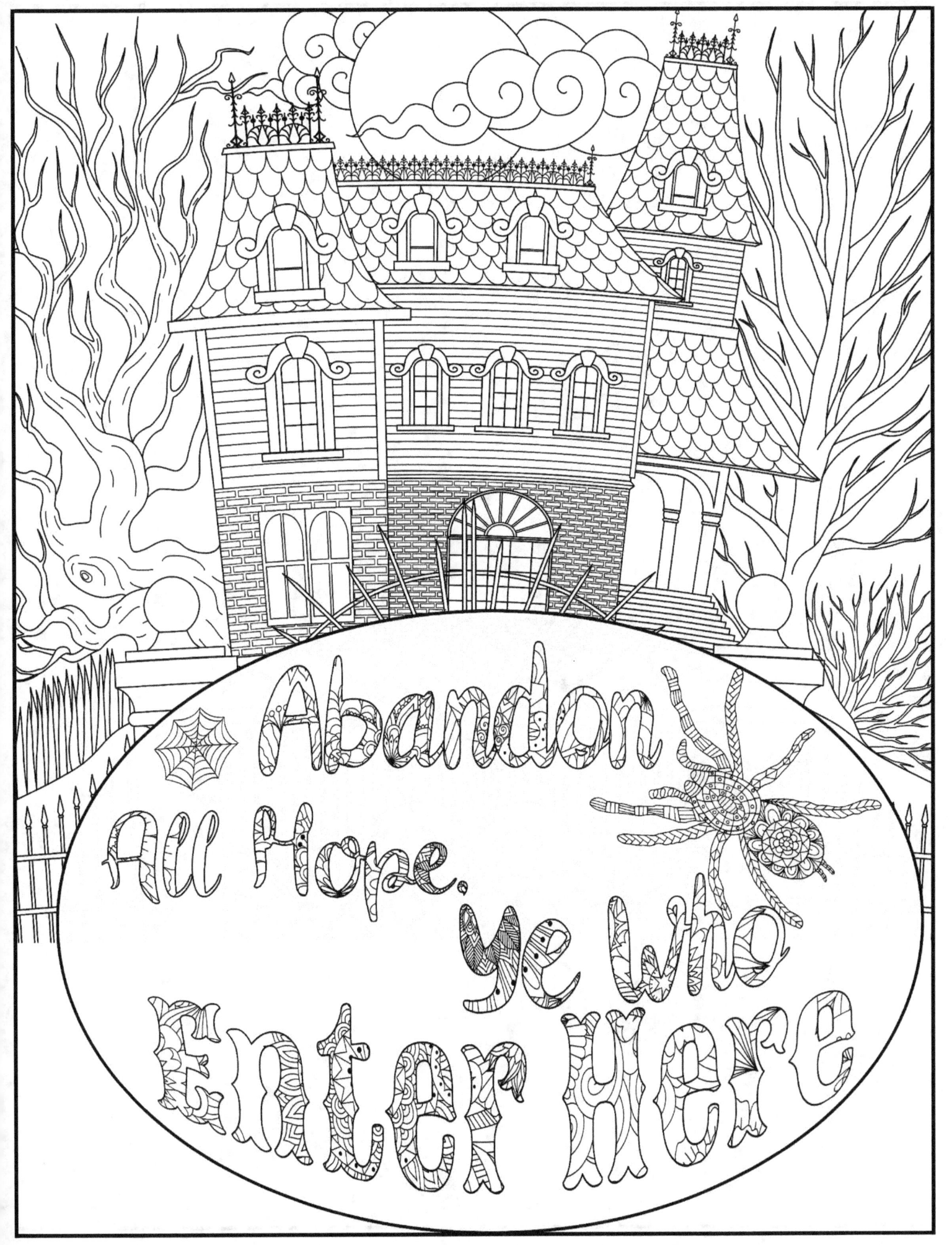

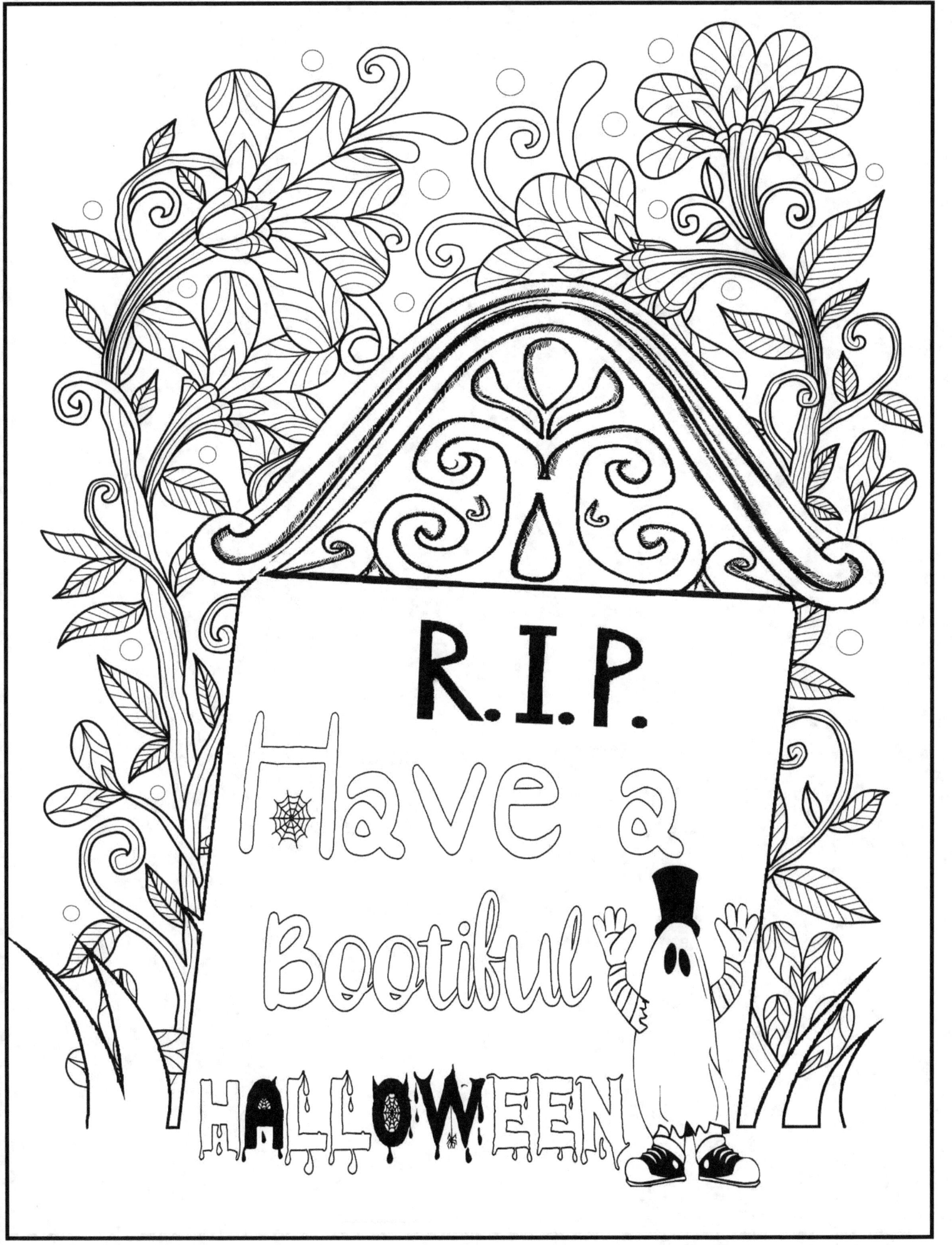

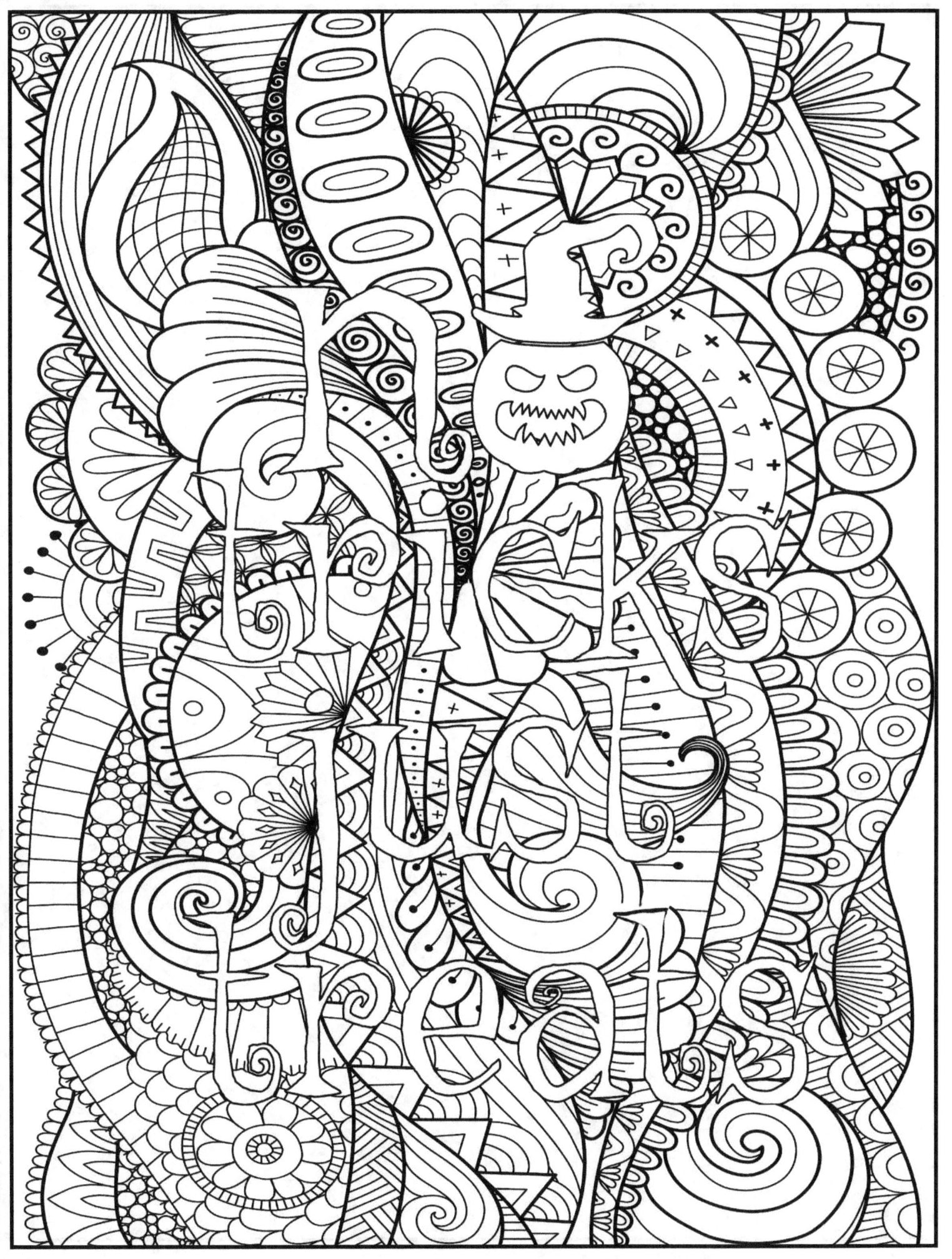

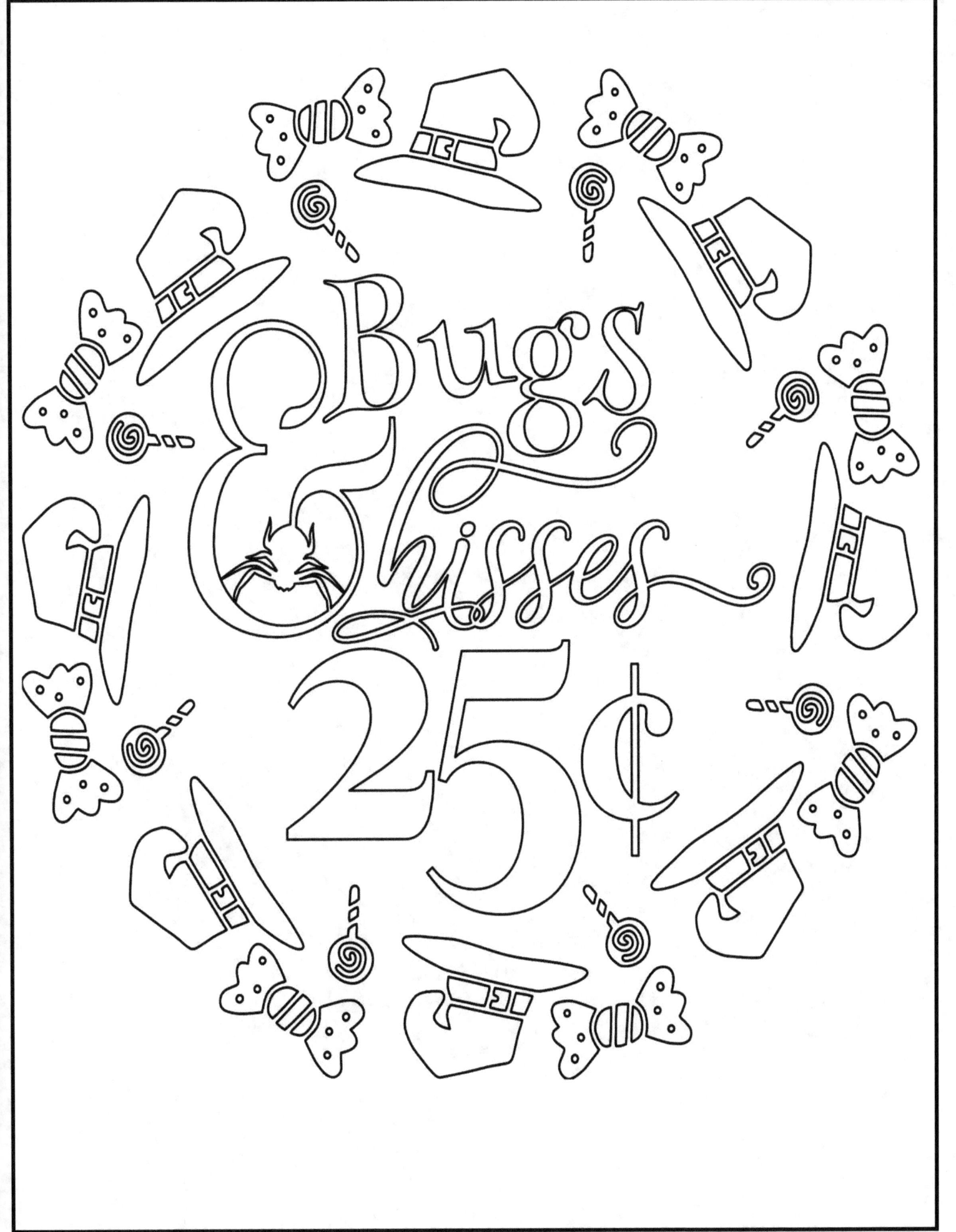

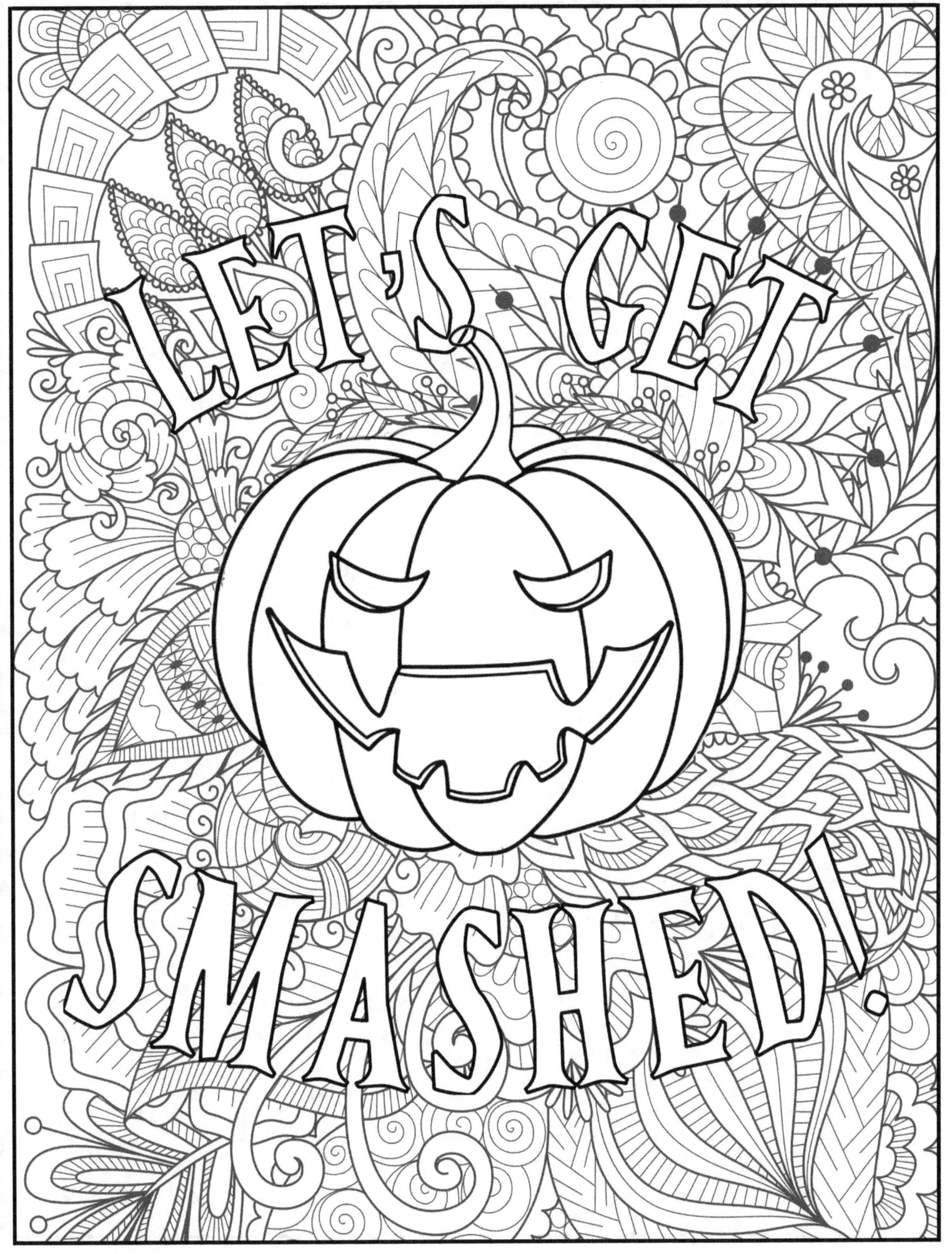

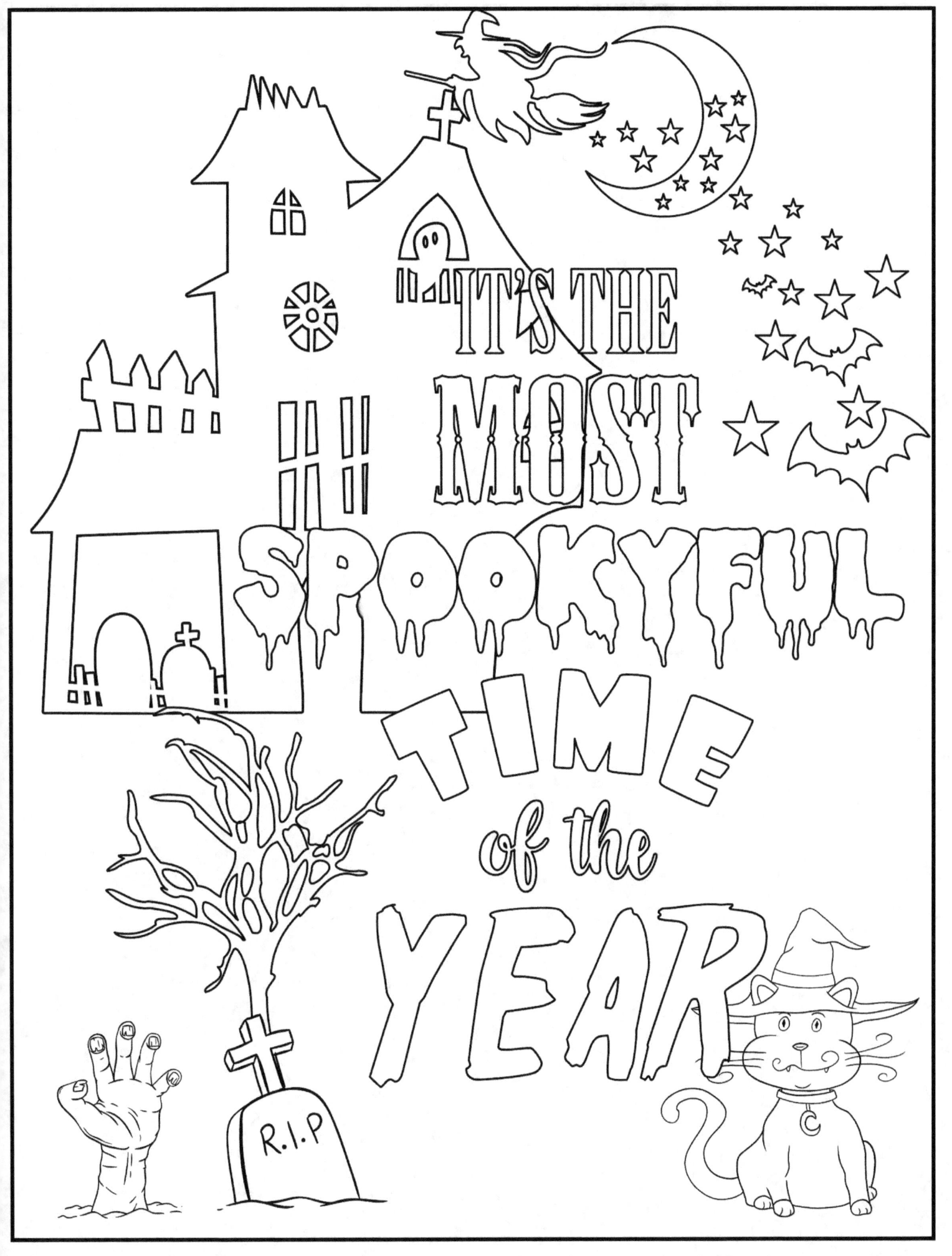

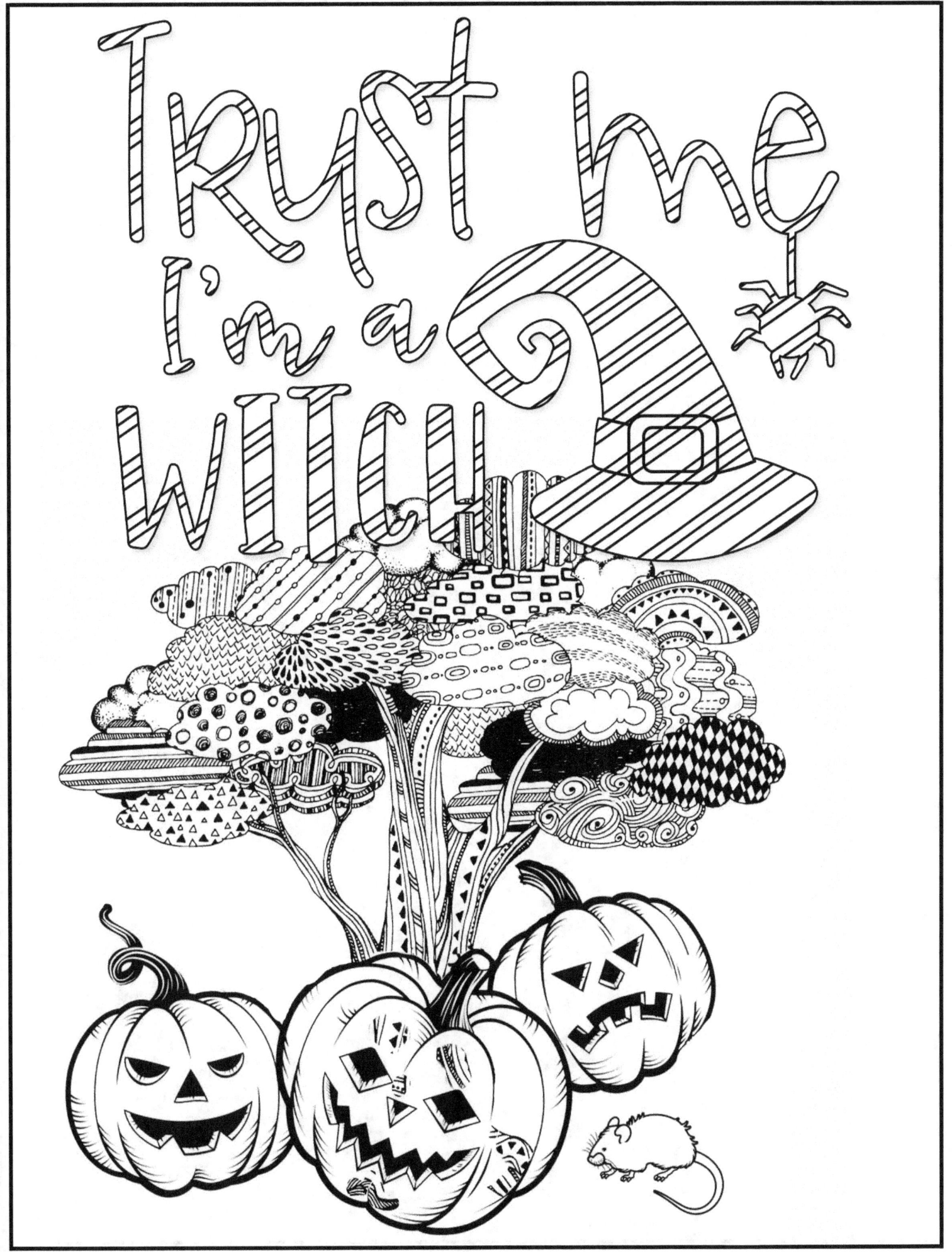

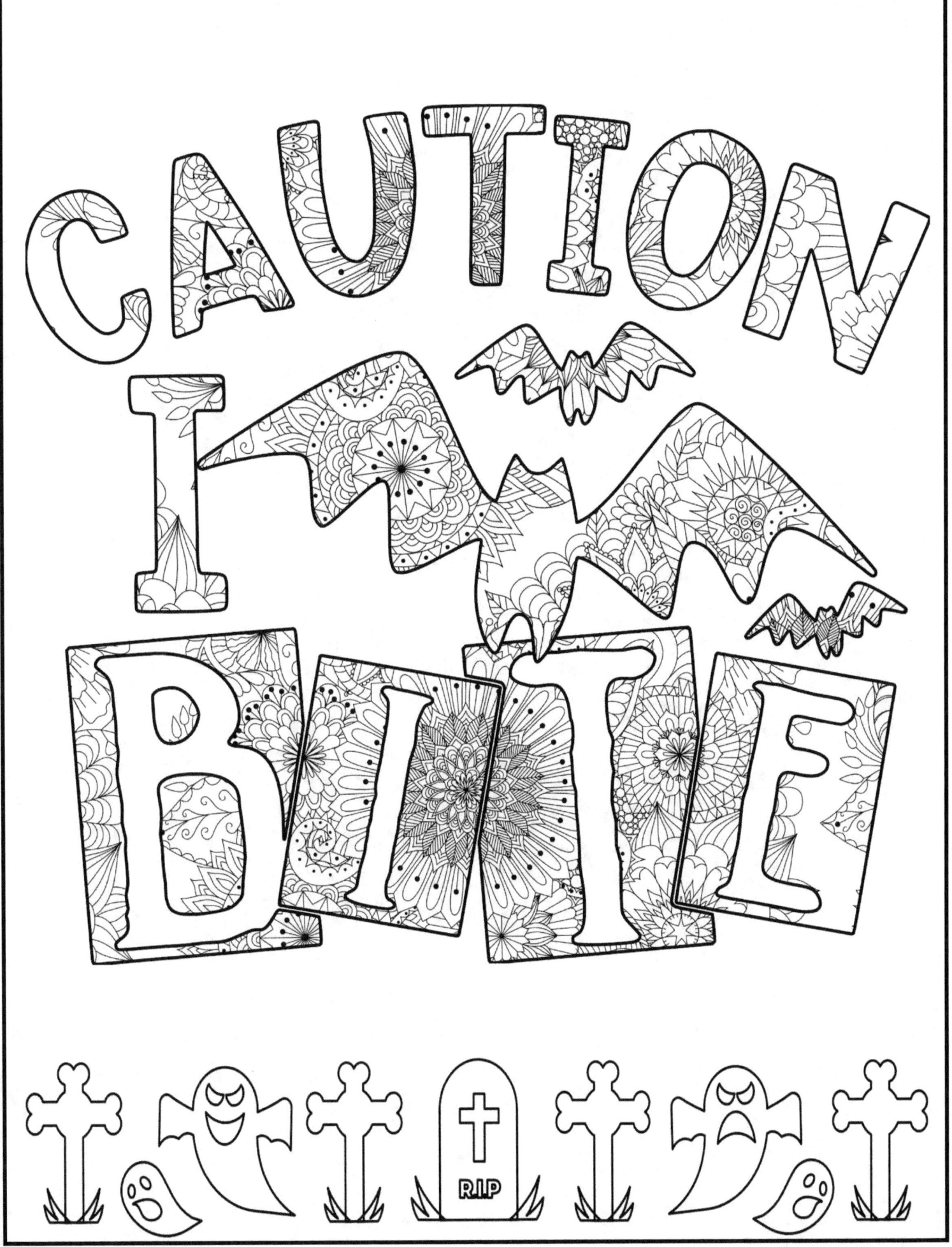

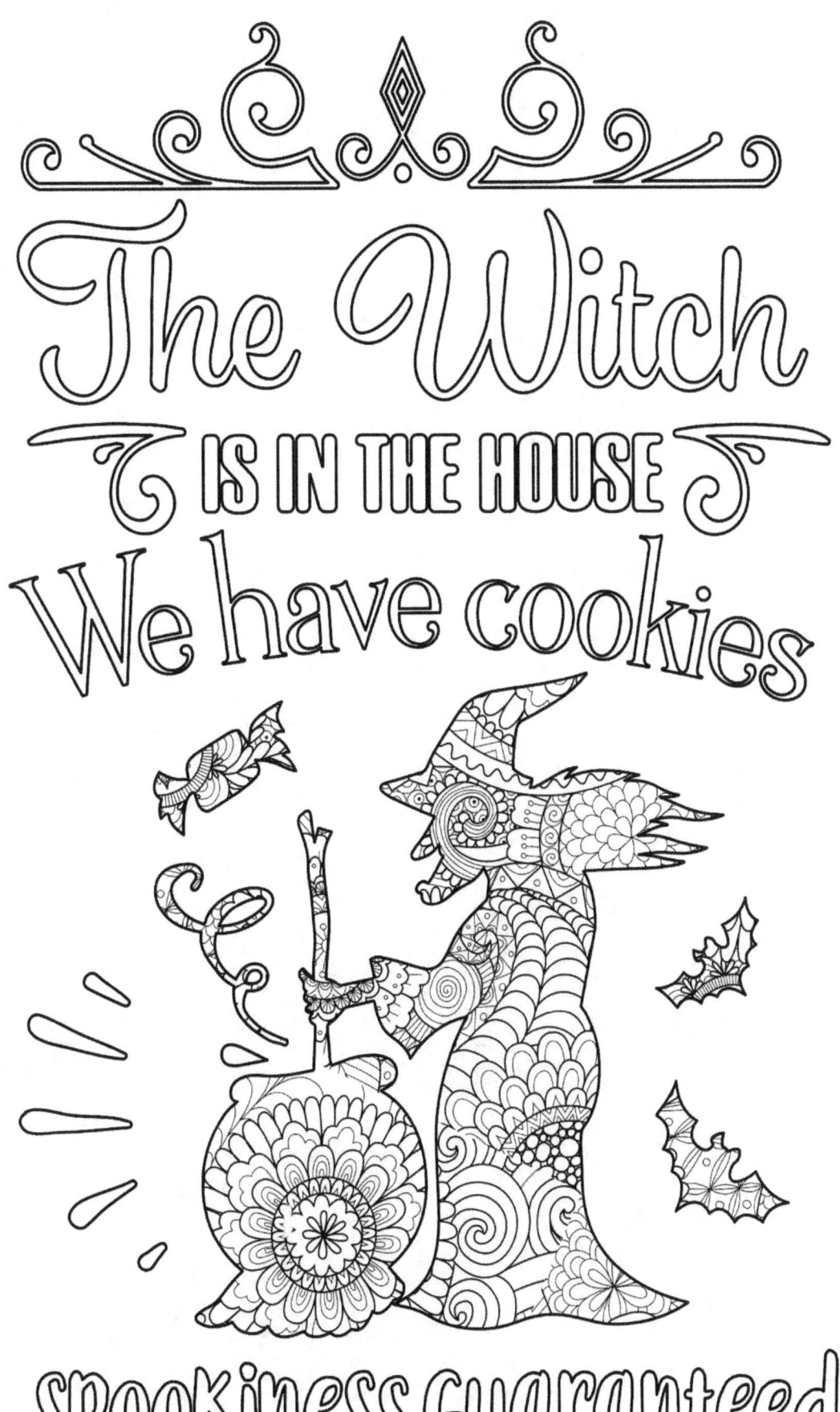

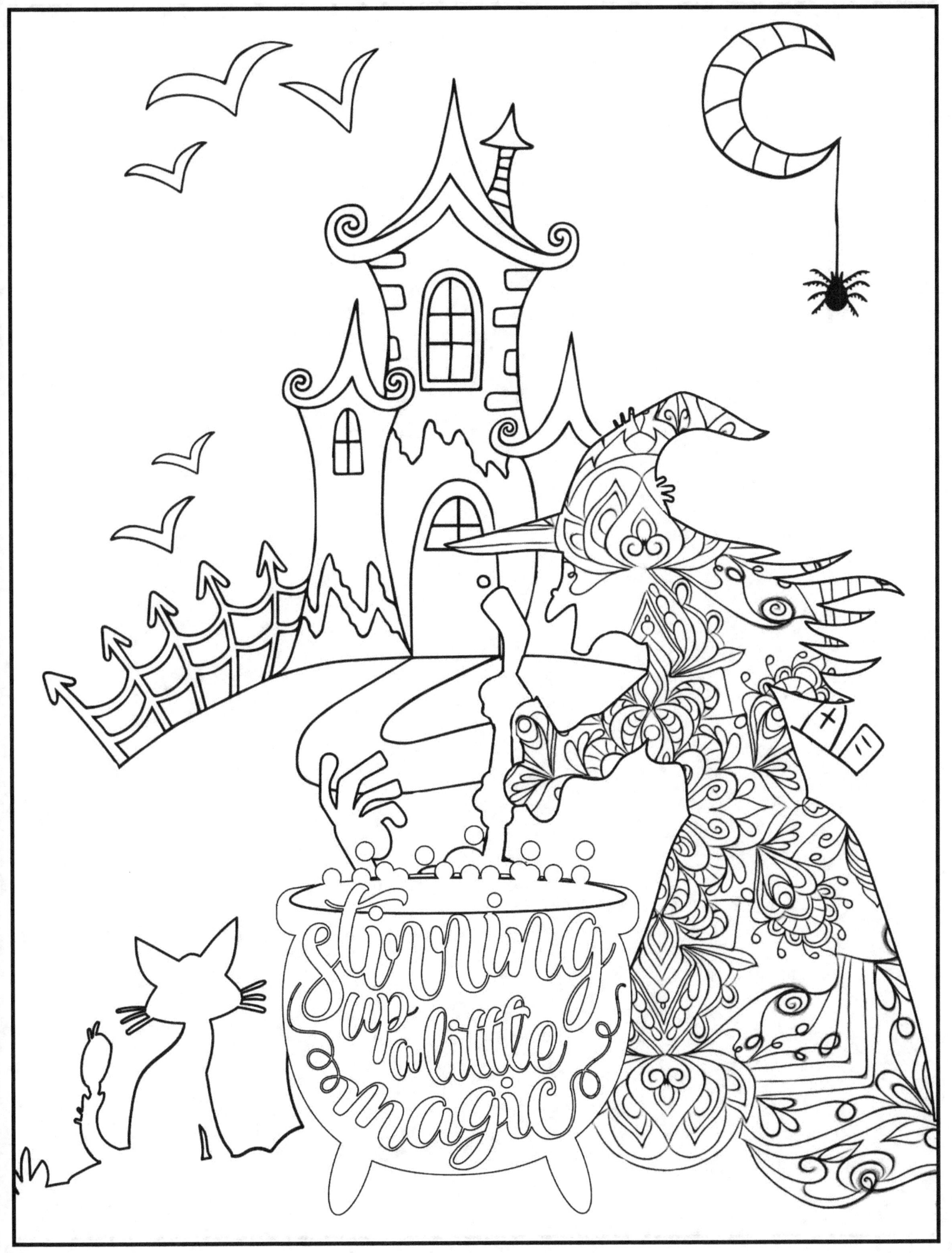

www.ingramcontent.com/pod-product-compliance
Lightning Source LLC
Chambersburg PA
CBHW080527220526
45465CB00006B/2626